Oc

Octopus pet Owner's book

Octopus book for pros and cons, tank, keeping, care, diet and health.

By

Diana Riffers

Table of Contents

Introduction

I want to thank you and congratulate you for buying the book 'Octopus as a pet'. This book will help you to understand everything you need to know about domesticating an Octopus. You will learn all the aspects related to keeping the animal successfully at home. You will be able to understand the pros and cons, behaviour, basic care, breeding, keeping, housing, diet and health issues related to the animal.

If you wish to own an octopus or even if you already own one, it is important to understand the basic characteristics of the animal. You should know what you can expect from the animal and what you can't. This will help you to tweak the way you behave with the octopus in the household, which in turn will help to build a strong bond between the pet and you.

Domestication of an animal has its unique challenges and issues. If you are not ready for these challenges, then you are not ready to domesticate the animal. It is important that you understand that owning any pet will have its advantages and disadvantages.

A pet is like a family member. You will be more like a parent than like a master to the pet. You will be amazed to see how much love and affection your Octopus will give through his ways and actions. But, for that to happen you have to make sure that the animal is taken care of. The animal should be loved in your household. If your family is not welcoming enough for the pet, the animal will lose its sense of being very quickly.

The diet of the Octopus will have a direct effect on the way he feels and functions. As the owner of the pet, it will be your responsibility that the pet is fed the right food in the right amounts and at the right times. You will also have to make sure that the pet is safe and secure at all times. It is important that you learn about the common health issues that the Octopus is likely to suffer from. This will help you to avoid these health conditions and keep the Octopus safe.

If the Octopus does not feel wanted and loved in your home, you will see a decline not just in its behaviour but also its health. This is the last thing that you should do to an animal. An animal deserves as much love and protection as a human being. You should be able to provide the pet a safe and sound home. Your family should be caring towards the pet. This is the basic requirement when planning to bring an animal home.

If you have already bought an Octopus, even then you need to understand your pet so that you take care of him in a better way. You should see whether with all its pros and cons, the animal fits well into your household. Domesticating and taming a pet is not only fun. There is a lot of hard work that goes into it.

Once you form a relationship with the octopus, it gets better and easier for you as the owner. The pet will be intelligent and adorable. He will also value the bond as much as you do. This will be good for the pet and also for you as the pet owner in the long run. It is important that you are ready to commit before you decide to domesticate the animal. If you are a prospective buyer, then understanding of these points will help you to make a wise decision.

When you bring a pet home, it becomes your responsibility to raise the pet in the best way possible. You have to provide physically, mentally, emotionally and financially for the pet. All these points are not being discussed to frighten or scare you. In fact, these points are being discussed to make you understand that you have to know the right ways to domesticate a pet. If the animal establishes a trust factor with you, he will always remain loyal to you. This is a great quality to have in a domesticated animal.

The pet will actually surprise you with their intelligence and smartness. This makes the pet all the more endearing. His unique ways and antics will leave you and the entire family in splits. If you have had a bad day, your pet will surely help you to release all the tension and enjoy life. If you are looking for a pet that is affectionate, lovable and fun, then the Octopus is the ideal choice for you as they won't disappoint you.

If you are looking forward to raise an Octopus as a pet, there are many things that you need to understand before you can domesticate the animal. You need to make sure that you are ready in terms of right preparation. There are certain unique characteristics of the animal that make him adorable, but these traits can also be very confusing for many people. You can't domesticate the animal with all the confusions in your head.

There are still many doubts regarding their domestication methods and techniques. There are many things that the prospective owners don't understand about the animal. They find themselves getting confused as to what should be done and what should be avoided. If you are still contemplating whether you wish to buy an Octopus or not, then it is important that you understand all about the maintenance of the pet, so that you can make the right choice for yourself. This book will help you make that decision.

This book is meant to equip you with all the knowledge that you need to have before buying the Octopus and bringing it home. This book will help you understand the basic behaviour and antics of the animal. You will also learn of various tricks and tips. These tips and tricks will be a quick guide when you are looking for different ways to have fun with your pet.

It is important that a prospective buyer has all the important information regarding an Octopus. You need to make sure that you are ready in terms of right preparation. This book will help you in this preparation and be a better owner for your pet.

You will learn many ways to take care of your Octopus. This book will try to address every question that you might have when looking at raising the animal. You will be able to understand the pet and give it the care that it requires.

You can expect to learn the pet's basic behaviour, aquarium needs, eating habits, shelter requirements, breeding, grooming and training techniques among other important things. In short, the book will help you to be a better owner by learning everything about the animal. This will help you form an everlasting bond with the pet.

Chapter 1: About the Octopus

An octopus is an eight armed, soft bodied Octopoda. Octopuses are bilaterally symmetric. This means that they have two eyes. They also have a beak to carry on some important life functions. The mouth is placed at the centre of the arms.

It should be noted here that various species of the Octopus are known to inhabit different parts of the ocean such as the pelagic water and coral reefs.

Previously, people hesitated to domesticate these beautiful animals. The main reason for this was that not much information was available about these animals. There were too many doubts in the minds of people, and there was no source to clear these doubts.

But now, it has become easier for people to learn more about these animals and domesticate them. The adorable octopuses are slowly becoming the most sought after pets. These animals are very different and unique as pets.

The Octopuses are slowly becoming more popular as pets. They are very attractive and people love to keep them at home. They look unlike any other pet animal. They can be great pets if you learn to domesticate them well.

While you might be extremely upbeat about bringing an Octopus home, it is necessary that you fully understand the pros and cons of getting the animal home. Even if you bring a dog home, you have to make sure that you are all ready for the responsibilities ahead. The dog is an easy to keep animal; still its maintenance requires certain efforts from you.

A pet is like a family member. You have to make sure that the animal is taken care of. The animal should be loved in your household. If your family is not welcoming enough for the pet, the animal will lose its sense of being very quickly.

You will see a decline not just in its behaviour but also its health. You should be able to provide the pet a safe and sound home. This is the basic requirement when planning to bring an animal home.

If an easily domesticated animal requires so much effort and attention on the part of the owner, then imagine how much effort a cephalopod would want? This is not to scare you, but to make you understand that you have to know the right ways to hand raise an Octopus. 7

An Octopus is a predominantly wild and marine animal. It is found in the open and the wild. There is a certain life style that the animal is accustomed to. You should be able to give the animal a space that does not disturb its normal lifestyle.

1. Scientific classification

Kingdom – The Animalia

Phylum – The mollusca

Class – The Cephalopoda

Sub class – The Coleoidea

Order – The Octopoda

Family – The Octopodidae

Subfamily – The Octopodinae

Genus – The Octopus

The Octopus is grouped under the Cephalopod class and Octopoda order. The genus is further divided into many species which you will learn in another section.

2. Cephalopods

Cephalopod is a name to classify animals that are head footed. Various animals such as the Octopus, cuttlefish and squid are grouped under cephalopods. They are classified as a class of mollusks. It should be noted that cephalopods further are grouped under two subclasses.

Cephalopods are very popular in many parts of the world. They have gained popularity as a major food source. They are fished extensively, yet are safe from the issue of overfishing. Cephalopods have a high reproductive rate. They can multiply very fast. So, even when they are being caught all over the world, they are safe as a species.

3. Life span

An Octopus has a short life span. It can live for 5-6 years. The key is to provide them the right environment and also the right nutrition. This will help them to grow, stay healthy and live longer.

It is also important to note that Octopuses are susceptible to viruses and bacteria. Once an Octopus gets a dangerous and life threatening infection, it can be very difficult to cure him.

The pet Octopus will require you to pay a lot of attention to its health, be it food choices or health care. The pet will definitely live longer if you make sure that you do all that is necessary for its health.

4. Species

It should be noted that more than 300 species of Octopus have been identified. These species have been grouped under the cephalopods class.

All these species are bilaterally symmetric. This means that they have two eyes. They also have a beak to carry on some important life functions.

5. Description and Taxonomy

These animals are said to be epibenthic. They are also pelagic in nature. The Incirrata group does not have any fins. It is also important to note that these animals also do not have cirri.

The Incirrata group animals are said to be shallow water epipelagic. They can also be moderately deep. This is one of the main things that distinguish them from the other main group.

Once you learn about the Incirrata group, it is also important to learn about the other major group which is the Cirrata group. This group lacks a supported fishery.

It should be noted here that only one out of the given eight families of this group is of some commercial use. This particular family is the concern for most aquarists.

It should be noted here that various species of the Octopus are known to inhabit different parts of the ocean such as the pelagic water and coral reefs.

6. Life history

The Octopus is further categorized to different species. It is known that there exist three hundred main species of the Octopus. These species are typically found in the open country areas where the water is not fully covered by scrubs.

There are further many sub species of the Octopus. The Octopus belonging to the main class can be found in rocky areas because such places provide them the necessary shade. The males of this species are known to reach a good weight.

The males are very opportunistic and have no seasonal mating traits. The life span of the animals of this species is around five years. They prefer being in the wild. But, they adapt very easily. They can survive well even in dry areas.

7. Understanding body functions of an octopus

Octopuses have no bones and are soft bodied, the bag shaped mantle on the dorsal part of the Octopus contains the internal organs and is commonly reddish brown in colour, usually darker in males than in females.

Chromatophores are highly developed pigment filled cells with radial muscles which enable the cell to rapidly expand and contract. This allows dramatic instantaneous changes of colour and pattern.

Colour changes can range from pale grey to dark brown, to dark red and to complement and enhance these, the Octopus is also able to change the texture of its skin from smooth to bumpy and spiny, even horned, through the activity of circular muscles.

The Octopus has highly developed senses that enable many of the extraordinary abilities characteristic to these creatures. Each of the 8 arms (in four pairs) possess up to 280 individual suction cups distributed in two rows, these contain thousands of chemical receptors used for taste and smell along with areas around the outer edge of the suckers that are sensitive to touch.

The suction cups are also able to rotate and move independently of the other suckers. These abilities allow the Octopus to distinguish between objects through touch alone, a skill particularly utilised when groping for prey in small dark spaces. In addition to this they also have the most developed eye and visual ability of all the invertebrates.

The Octopuses are generally considered to be the most intelligent invertebrate animals and have the most complex brain, with the capacity for both long and short term memory. As such, these creatures are able to solve and remember puzzles and problems through trial and error and experience.

8. Biological Information

Biological information includes species composition, size (weight, DML, TL), sex and state of reproductive maturity. Two species (O. dofleini and O. rubescens) may be included in landings from the shrimp trawl and trap fisheries.

Any Octopus over 500g can be safely assumed to be O. dofleini, and any mature Octopus less than 500g can safely be assumed to be O. rubescens. Other characters useful for discerning the two species are provided.

Mass is an appropriate measure of a living Octopus. However, for accurate weights, care must be taken to drain the mantle cavity of water. DML or TL is variable, dependent upon state of mantle contraction and muscular contraction of the limbs.

For commercial size Octopuses, sex is easily determined externally through examination of the third right arm for a hectocotylus. If the third arm is missing or damaged, sex can be determined by internal examination.

The reproductive glands and ducts of the female are paired, while the male develops a spermatic duct, penis and diverticulum on the left side. In Octopus vulgaris, the sexes can be determined internally at hatching. External differentiation of the hectocotylus does not begin to develop on males until they are 50-70g in weight.

9. Geographic Range

An Octopus can be found all in kinds of coral reefs. They are found even in the cold waters of the coast. You can easily find them in northern temperate areas, pacific regions and south California.

Alaska and Korea are also known to be great reservoirs of the Octopus. It should be noted that these places can be utilized as areas to rest and feed.

They also act as places to protect from various predators such as orca, sea otters and sperms whales. It should also be noted that these areas also serve as good chambers from brooding.

10. Conservation

There is little information on the population conservation status, though it is not currently considered threatened. This species is fished commercially; cephalopods have long been a valuable human food source with an estimated 3 million tonnes of cephalopods caught globally each year.

For centuries, Giant Pacific Octopuses have been targeted by fishermen for food and as bait for halibut fishing off the west coast of Canada and America. Around Vancouver the annual landings of octopus have fluctuated widely – they averaged less than 22 tonnes until 1987, then increased to 200 tonnes in the late 1980s when demand for halibut bait increased.

The fishery reached a peak in 1997 at 217 tonnes-118 tonnes from the dive fishery and 99 tonnes from the trap and trawl fishery, but landings decreased to 26 tonnes in 2005. Demand for Octopus as bait declined when halibut quota was assigned on an individual basis, which made the fishery less competitive.

There is anecdotal evidence that the number of extremely large GPOs being spotted and caught in Canadian waters has decrease in the last 50 years but this is difficult to back up with concrete evidence. The sheer size of the coastline and the low density of the human population along it make the current level of fishing sustainable.

Catching Giant Pacific Octopus is not easy, modern fisheries today include trap and dive fisheries as well as a limited by-catch trawl fishery. Catching giant Octopus in mobile fishing gear such as bottom trawls is fairly unusual as they tend to stay around rocky sea beds, which snag on mobile gear.

They also are not likely to be caught in monofilament fishing lines as they don't tangle easily and find it relatively easy to escape. Crab pots can be dangerous to GPOs but in most cases they are able to escape before the pots are hauled.

Studies of fishing impact on the Octopus species suggest that the reproductive strategy of Octopuses make them far less vulnerable to overfishing. The short period of time before juvenile Octopus reach maturity and produce a large number of offspring allows populations to recover far more rapidly than many other marine species.

Over-fishing of other species has resulted in reduced predation on GPO's, reduced competition for invertebrate prey and may explain stable catch per unit effort data collected on Octopus stocks around the Hokkaido island of Northern Japan. Populations in shallow waters are likely to be vulnerable to habitat threats resulting from human activities, being particularly sensitive to pollution.

No protection is provided under CITES or IUCN Red list legislation and there are no current targeted conservation actions, though populations of this species are known from several North American Marine National Parks.

Chapter 2: Things you should know before you buy an Octopus

If you wish to own an Octopus or even if you already own one, it is important to understand the basic characteristics of the animal. You should know what you can expect from the animal and what you can't.

This will help you to tweak the way you behave with the Octopus in the household, which in turn will help to build a strong bond between the pet animal and you.

Octopuses are known to be very loyal animals. If they establish a trust factor with you, they will always remain loyal to you. This is a great quality to have in a domesticated animal.

Along with being loyal, they are also known to possess great intelligence. They will actually surprise you with their intelligence.

When the Octopus is in a happy mood, he will jump around the entire space of the aquarium. His unique ways and antics will leave you and the entire family in splits. If you have had a bad day, your pet will surely help you to release all the tension and enjoy life.

They are also very entertaining and playful. You can expect the entire household to be entertained by the unique gimmicks and pranks of the Octopus. If you are looking for a pet that is affectionate, lovable and fun, then this animal is the ideal choice for you as they won't disappoint you.

In spite of all the qualities of the Octopus, it is often termed as a high maintenance pet. If you are still contemplating whether you wish to buy an Octopus or not, then it is important that you understand all about the maintenance of the pet, so that you can make the right choice for yourself.

1. Copper toxicity in cephalopods

There is a lot of confusion whether copper is toxic to the cephalopods or not. Many people believe that a small amount of copper must be available in oceans. Most pipes that carry water to tanks also have copper. This could mean that copper is not toxic to cephalopods.

But, this is not true. Copper is toxic for the cephalopods. The issue of copper toxicity to cephalopods is a matter of dissolved copper in the water out-competing the copper in the blood for oxygen.

2. Intelligent animals

It is known that Octopuses are very intelligent. In fact, it is said that they are most intelligent amongst all the invertebrates, such as insects and worms. An Octopus has many qualities that were earlier believed to be a domain of the vertebrates.

An Octopus has many cognitive, affective and behavioural abilities that make it similar to even the higher vertebrates. For example, you shouldn't be surprised if you notice an Octopus holding a wine bottle and then eventually removing its cork. There are many octopuses that open boxes and jars easily.

Many researches and scientists have noticed and documented their experiences and learning about the Octopus. During one such research, Roland Andersen from Seattle Aquarium shared some of his unique experiences.

According to Roland Andersen, Octopuses can spit on the face of a person. He saw Octopuses spit on the faces of many scientists. This revelation only strengthens the belief that Octopuses have the ability to surprise you, even shock you.

There are people who have documented their experiences with the Octopus. Many people pet them when they play with them. This is generally done on the back of the Octopus. They display a playful behaviour at such times.

The Octopuses are generally considered to be the most intelligent invertebrate animals and have the most complex brain, with the capacity for both long and short term memory.

There have also been reports that prove that the Octopus can use available tools to guard itself. During an experiment it was seen that the Octopus was keeping a coconut shell that it found as a guarding tool.

It was observed that the pet kept its eight arms around the coconut to guard itself. The coconut shell gave the pet a feeling of safety and security.

The Octopus can be very moody. You will observe that the same animal has the capacity to sometimes be extremely playful at times and laidback at other times. This animal can be very aggressive, also.

You should understand that domesticating any kind of pet is a long term commitment. Once you have brought the pet home, you have to help him adjust to the new surroundings. You should make the entire process gradual so that it is simpler for the pet.

An animal that is given a new environment will get stressed very easily. This will further make the transitioning more difficult. You should start focusing on bonding with your pet so that he does not get all flustered and stressed.

It is suggested that a routine should be followed. Take out some time every day for your pet animal. Follow some tasks every single day and you will notice the pet getting comfortable with you.

Don't worry if the pet is a little reserved initially. He will slowly get used to you being around and will associate it with security. This will help the two of you to bond well.

3. Habitat requirements of the Octopus

It is very important that you understand the habitat requirements of the Octopus. If you can't provide your pet a habitat that keeps him happy and safe, then you will fail as the parent of the pet. You need to make sure that the pet gets what would make it happy.

Every animal is so used to its own natural surroundings that as the owner of a new invertebrate, you should make sure that you fulfil the habitat requirements of your pet animal. But before you can do so for your pet Octopus, you should be able to understand what your Octopus needs.

In the first few weeks of your Octopus, you need to be more careful as everything will be new for the pet. He will take time to get used to the new environment.

It is necessary that the infant spends as much time as possible with you. You should treat the Octopus as your own infant baby. This is the time when you will form a bond with your pet.

But as your pet grows and matures, it needs some extra physical space for itself. It will need the space to grow and move around. In their natural habitat, Octopuses are used to a lot of space. So, you should be able to give them the desired space even in your home. As the Octopus grows, it would like to have a good amount of space for himself.

Designing the right water tank is very essential when domesticating an Octopus. It is important that the enclosure is built by keeping the following points in mind:

The enclosure space should be enough for the animal. You should take into consideration that the Octopus will grow and mature with time and accordingly his needs will change.

As the Octopus grows, it will require more and more space. The space that you provide him should not restrict him in any way.

It should be kept as real and natural as possible. You can't keep a bird cage in a setting that is meant to be for a dog. There are specific needs for each animal, even for their habitats. It is important that you understand the habitat requirements of the Octopus.

The Octopus should feel comfortable and easy in the enclosure. The structure and furnishing should resemble his natural habitat. This will make the animal feel as if it is in its natural home in the wild.

The enclosure should be built in a way that is predator proof. The enclosure should be able to provide the necessary protection and safety.

You should make an in-depth analysis of the various predators that could attack the pet animal in his enclosure. You should plan the safety measures keeping in mind the strength of the predators.

The enclosure also needs to be escape proof. What if your pet decides to just escape from a gap in the enclosure? Make sure the enclosure is designed and built keeping in mind this particular point.

The enclosure should make the Octopus emotionally safe. He needs to feel safe and secure in the setting. He needs to be comfortable and happy.

These pets are easily prone to stress. So, you should make sure that the enclosure should give him the space to de-stress and relax.

The water tank you build will depends on the space that you can afford to have. If you have no space constraints then you should make a bigger tank for the animal. It is known that the bigger the habitat is, the better it is for the animal. These animals are very active and thus more space is always a blessing for them.

4. Legal regulations and fishing for Octopuses

Giant Pacific Octopuses can be acquired from licensed collectors in the USA, Canada and Japan. Divers capture Octopus to order, usually small specimens are preferred as they acclimate better to captive conditions and have a longer life expectancy in captivity.

Fish anaesthetics, MS222 or Quinaldine in alcohol, are used to flush the Octopus out of its lair and once in open water it is wrestled into a plastic fish bag. In the past collectors used chlorine solutions and even copper sulphate but although working well they obviously harmed the specimens and surrounding invertebrates considerably.

Hydrogen peroxide is now used by a lot of collectors (Anderson 1995), this would annoy the Octopus, but as hydrogen peroxide rapidly breaks down to water and oxygen it is less damaging. It is extremely rare for a GPO to react aggressively when being collected – in 30 years of collecting in Canadian waters Phillip Bruecker says he has never been attacked but a colleague Doug Pemberton is featured with one trying to grab him repeatedly on a YouTube video.

Octopuses should be handled carefully to ensure no damage is caused to their delicate skin. To move an Octopus from one tank to another the best way is to spend some time getting the Octopus used to human interaction.

Once they associate humans with food and play they enjoy interacting and will usually come straight over to the edge of the tank – it is then relatively easy to net them in a soft net or scoop them into a fish bag or bucket. I have moved young active GPO's in this way many times and have even been able to lift them out of the water into a large bucket as they grip onto you very firmly if they are in the mood.

Moving a grumpy senescent Octopus can be more difficult as they tend to hold fast onto the rocks/hide in their lair. In this case it is often easiest to drain the tank and once they are exposed to air they are more likely to let go of the rocks and as they slip down towards the water you can manhandle them (firmly but gently) into a suitable bongo or large bucket.

Japan

Most literature related to Octopuses and Octopus fisheries in Japan dates back to the 1960's and 1970's. Two recent references are reviews of cephalopod fisheries that deal with octopus only briefly. Japanese Octopus fisheries primarily target O. vulgaris in the south and O. dofleini in the north.

Other species fished include O. araneoides, O. conspadiceus, O. cyanea, O. membranaceus, O. minor and O. ocellatus (Osako and Murata 1983; Okutani 1990).

The fishery for giant Pacific Octopus occurs primarily off Hokkaido and off northern Honshu. Two other species, O. conspadiceus and O. areneoides are a minor component of landings from these areas.

North West Africa

The Saharan trawl fishery for cephalopods developed through the late 1950's and 1960's as Japanese and Spanish trawlers depleted stocks of sea bream (Family Sparidae) and switched to increased abundance of Octopus (O. vulgaris), cuttlefishes (Sepia officinalis officinalis, S. officinalis herredda, S. bertheloti, S. elegans and S. orbignyana) and squid (Loligo vulgaris and L. forbesi) (Bravo de Laguna 1989).

The fishery occurs on three main fishing grounds between 13 and 28°N, off the coasts of Morocco, Mauritania, Senegal, Gambia and Guinea Bissau, with the major production coming from FAO Area, between 19 and 26°N.

It is a multinational fishery involving vessels from Japan, Spain, Morocco, Korea, Mauritania, and, to a lesser extent, Libya, Italy, Soviet Union, Greece, Panama and Taiwan. Octopuses accounted for between 67,000 and 128,000 mt.

Mexico

A mother ship-based drift line fishery for Octopus Maya has been carried out since 1949 off the Yucatan Peninsula on the Caribbean coast of Mexico (Solis-Ramirez 1997). Mother ship vessels support canoes or flat-bottomed skiffs which fish Octopuses using baited lines attached to bamboo poles.

The smaller (18-31 ft) artisanal fleet conducts day trips with 1-3 boats per mother ship, and may land as much as 200 kg per trip. The larger (40-72 ft) mechanized fleet makes trips of 12 or more days with 5-7 skiffs per mother ship, and may land up to 11 tons per trip.

The fishery produced between 1,412 and 8,933 mt per year between 1970 and 1986. Maya is a relatively large (60-250 mm ML) Octopus which occupies a relatively small geographic distribution surrounding the Yucatan Peninsula, at depths to 50 in (van Heukelem 1983; Solis-Ramirez 1997). It is a large-egged species which lacks a planktonic paralarval stage.

5. Transportation

Giant Pacific Octopuses are regularly shipped to Europe from Canada via air in insulated 'octo-barrels'. These are plastic food/liquid barrels with a sturdy lid held shut by a metal clamp, padded out with a generous layer of loft insulation. The Octopuses are starved for 10-14 days prior to shipment to ensure the water is not soiled too much.

Water is pre cooled before shipping to 3 degrees Celsius less than ambient temperature to ensure that the temperature stays cool for the transport. Heavy duty large fish bags are used to hold the specimen and the volume of water should be at least twice the volume of the Octopus.

The specimen should be triple bagged as it is not impossible for them to bite a hole in a bag; the bags filled with pure oxygen and knotted or tied using elastic bands or cable ties. The barrels should be insulated with rock wool loft insulation or similar and cold packs used to keep the temperature low during transit.

6. Display justification

Octopuses have long been hugely popular with visitors to public aquaria. Victorian naturalist and gentleman Henry Lee of Brighton aquarium famously stated that "An aquarium without an Octopus is like a plum-pudding without plums".

At Blue Reef Aquarium Newquay, the giant Pacific Octopus ranked as second most popular animal at the aquarium after sharks, beating seahorses, rays, turtles, clownfish and corals (visitor surveys between 2001 and 2011).

Interactive feeding demonstrations with the giant Octopus are the most popular talks of the day and of all the educational talks these receive the most positive comments in surveys. People are fascinated by these alien creatures and as a result of this attention grabbing creature aquarium staff are able to educate far more customers that otherwise would leave without a conservation message.

It is well known that the majority of aquarium visitors do not read signs but all are happy to listen to an engaging, interesting and short commentary from an enthusiastic biologist. As long as ethical considerations are fully addressed the keeping of this species has considerable benefits.

7. Capturing Octopuses

Various types of gear have been used to capture Octopuses, including pots, traps, trawls, snares, drift fishing, spearing, hooking and hand collection.

Pots or traps are open un-bated structures designed to collect Octopuses by exploiting their tendency to use such refuges between hunting activities or as brooding chambers.

Traps can also include baited structures with a closing lid or trapdoor to retain the Octopus after it enters to collect the bait. Trawls are funnel shaped nets held open by floats on the head rope and either a beam on the footrope or a pair of doors, which is pulled across the bottom behind a vessel.

Snares are long lines suspended off the bottom with an array of bare hooks on gang ions forming a curtain across the bottom. Drift fishing uses hand lines and baited lures which are dragged across the bottom by a drifting boat or individual floats.

When an Octopus seizes the lure, the line tightens, the fisher retrieves the line, removes and kills the Octopus, and resets the line. Spearing and hooking of the Octopus is done either from a small boat or wading in shallow water.

Octopuses encountered in the open are speared, and hooks are used to remove the Octopus from dens. Hand collection is accomplished by driving an Octopus from its den with a chemical irritant with the help of bleach, vinegar, fresh water and capturing it by hand.

This is done by divers or in the intertidal zone. Octopuses are frequently taken incidentally in fisheries for other species, and in some fisheries are considered nuisance species.

There are a number of ways to collect Octopuses. One of the easiest and most fun is to go tide pooling during low tide at night. Night snorkelling, night diving, and laying trap lines of pots (artificial dens) may also work.

Keep in mind that Octopuses have an arsenal of tricks at their disposal. They can change colour, change skin texture, move through very small holes, produce an ink decoy, and jet. After you have collected an Octopus, keep an eye on her or him and be prepared to do a water change if the Octopus inks in a small volume of water.

Also keep in mind that Octopuses are notorious escape artists. If you plan to collect an Octopus and are not familiar with their special needs, you need to be more prepared. It is better to prepare well than to regret later.

Various examples include: Eledone cirrhosa in the Scottish fishery for lobsters (Nephrops norevegicus and Homarus vulgaris); Octopus vulgaris in the English Channel fishery for H. vulgaris and the Florida stone crab (Menippe mercenaria) fishery; O. maorum in a New Zealand fishery for rock lobsters (Jasus edwardsii and J. verreauxi); O. tetricus and O. flindersi in Australian fisheries for rock lobsters (Panulirus longipes cygnus and Janus novaehollandiae); O. dofleini in northeastern Pacific crab (Cancer magister, Chionocetes bairdi and Paralithodes camtschatica) fisheries; and O. dofleini and O. rubescens in northeastern Pacific spot prawn (Pandalus platyceros) fisheries.

Three major experimental trap fisheries for Octopuses have been undertaken in British Columbia waters, one by DFO and two independent studies. An experimental trap fishery was carried out in Barkley Sound, Vancouver Island, in February and March 1979.

Wooden boxes, amphora pots, half-tire traps, paint and oil cans, pardiac prawn traps and igloo crab traps were used. A total of 1,432 traps were hauled, and these produced 9 Octopes, all less than 100g total weight. The traps (wooden box, crab and prawn traps and half-tires) were set between 7 and 66 in depth, and all were baited with either frozen herring or perforated tins of pet food.

In some cases, authorities have encouraged development of Octopus fisheries to reduce the number of predators and supplement the income of fishers.

Dive fisheries

Harvest log information for the Octopus dive fishery was first collected in 1983 with the introduction of the Z licence. Landings remained low up until 1987 when demand for Octopuses as halibut bait increased.

Between 1988 and 1990, reported landings reached 154 mt, but declined in 1991, possibly as a result of the introduction of individual vessel quotas in the halibut fishery. Landings remained relatively low up until 1996 with landings decreasing to 46.8 mt in 1995. In 1996 landings increased again reaching 76 .2 mt.

The Octopus dive fishery has traditionally taken place in the South Coast of B.C. due in large part to the close proximity of processing and freezer facilities. Harvest locations remain highly consistent from year to year, with the majority of landings taken from Statistical area.

Trap fisheries

There is virtually no trap or pot fishery directed specifically at Octopuses in places such as British Columbia. For the years 1992-96, the number of "Z-P" Octopuses by trap licences issued ranged from 161 to 233. Of these, the number that reported landings ranged from 68 to 141.

Examination of harvest log information produced only 8 fishers who landed Octopuses by trap who were not participants in either prawn and shrimp trap or crab trap fisheries. Because Octopus landings are recorded on separate logbooks, and data coders sometimes did not know which trap type was used to produce the catch.

Although fishing effort occurs primarily during fall and winter, monthly CPUE rates do not vary considerably by season. Monthly averages calculated over the last 14 years show only a small decrease during late spring and early summer.

8. Pros and cons of domesticating Octopuses

If you are in two minds whether you need an Octopus or not, then this section will make it simpler for you. You should objectively look at the various advantages and disadvantages of owning an Octopus. This will help you to make your decision.

It is important that you understand that owning any pet will have its advantages and disadvantages. You should see whether with all its pros and cons, the animal fits well into your household.

A few advantages and disadvantages of domestication of Octopuses have been discussed in this section. If you are a prospective buyer, then this section will help you to make a wise decision.

There are people who are impressed by the adorable looks of the Octopus. They think that this reason is enough to domesticate the animal. They believe that just because of the way the pet looks, it wouldn't require any maintenance. But, this is not true.

Domestication of an Octopus has its unique challenges and issues. If you are not ready for these challenges, then you are not ready to domesticate the animal. Once you understand the areas that would require extra work from your side, you will automatically give your very best in those areas.

If you have already bought an Octopus, even then this section will help you. The list of pros and cons of Octopuses will help you to prepare yourself for the challenges that lie ahead of you. This list will help you to be a better parent to the pet and to form an ever-lasting bond with your beloved pet.

Pros of domesticating an Octopus:

If you are still not sure about buying an Octopus or not, then you should know that there are many pros of domesticating this animal. They are loved by their owners and their families because of some amazing qualities that they possess.

This animal can definitely prove to be a great pet for your household and your family.

The various advantages of domesticating an Octopus are as follows:

-   The Octopus is considered to be a very intelligent pet. It is always great to have an intelligent pet. You will be surprised many a times by his intelligent behaviour.

-   An Octopus is easy to keep if all their conditions and requirements are met. It might take you some time to understand the temperament of the animal. And, once you are able to do so, it only gets easier from there.

-   Their looks make them different and adorable to look at. They are loved by one and all. Who wouldn't want to have a pet that is beautiful to look at?

-   If you care well for the pet, he will also respond in a very positive way. When the Octopus is in a happy mood, he will be stress free and relaxed. His unique ways and antics will leave you in splits.

-   The Octopus is very entertaining. If you just sit around the water tank, you are bound to have a great time.

-   If there are kids in your home, then they will fall in love with this pet. But, you should monitor the interaction of the kids with the pet. This is important to keep everyone safe and sound.

- The food that the Octopus thrives on is easily available. The Octopus needs food only once a day. This can be great news for people who worry about feeding a variety of food to their pets three times a day.

- The Octopuses are generally considered to be the most intelligent invertebrate animals and have the most complex brain, with the capacity for both long and short term memory.

- Many people pet them when they play with them. This is generally done on the back of the Octopus. They display a playful behaviour at such times.

- You can make a strong emotional bond with your pet and can enjoy the fruits of the bond for years to come.

- A very important point to note here is that their demeanour will depend a lot on how they are raised. The preparation has to begin right from the start. You can't expect them to suddenly become friendly after years of wrong treatment. If they are raised to be social, they will be very social.

- The Octopuses don't overeat, so you don't have to worry in this aspect. The Octopus will eat as much is required. They are used to eating small meals.

- One of your main concerns could be the diet of the pet. Even if you love your pet dearly, you would want to avoid any hassles while feeding the pet. You might not have the time to prepare special food all the time. In case you domesticate an Octopus, then you will not have to worry too much about the diet. The Octopus can be served meat with some store bought Octopus food. These are easily available food items to ensure that the right nutrition is given to your pet.

- This pet will be the centre of affection for all the family members and also for each and every visitor of the house.

- An Octopus has many cognitive, affective and behavioural abilities that make it similar to even the higher vertebrates.

- It is known that Octopuses are very intelligent.

- They are also very entertaining and playful. You can expect the entire household to be entertained by the unique gimmicks and pranks of the Octopus.

- Everybody in the house will love the pet. This is because of its very unique nature.

Cons of domesticating an Octopus:

While you have studied the advantages of domesticating an Octopus, it is also important to learn about the various disadvantages that come along. Everything that has merits will also have some demerits, and you should be prepared for this.

The adorable and friendly animal has his own set of challenges when it comes to domesticating them. It is important to understand these disadvantages so that you can be better prepared for them. Following are the disadvantages of raising an Octopus:

- The Octopuses are very energetic by nature. This behaviour could be difficult for a first time owner.

- These animals have a very unique temperament, and it would require patience from your side to understand this kind of temperament.

- Octopuses are capable of escaping. They are talented enough to do so. They can easily squeeze through a small gap. This gap needs to be a little larger than the beak, which is the only hard part of the Octopus.

- The Octopus can be very moody.

- You might have to take the decision to euthanize your pet Octopus. You might have to carry on a more elaborate procedure for older and bigger Octopuses. Bad health is generally one of the main reasons to conduct the procedure. Old age is also a very common reason to euthanize an animal. Once the Octopus is old and incapable, it can get very difficult for him.

- The pet will depend on you for most of its needs. You should be able to identify the symptoms of various diseases in your pet to treat it well.

- The Octopus can eat its own arms when it is in stress. This is self-cannibalism. It is very common in many species of Octopuses.

- If you are not careful or are inexperienced, they can lose their lives very easily.

- Kids can sometimes be very mischievous when in a playful mood. The child might just trying to be a little friendly or naughty, but the animal can get irritated. While many pet animals might not react to such an action, the Octopus can get angry and might even try to harm the kid.

- Male and female Octopuses lose their lives after mating. A male will die after a few months of mating, while a female will die soon after her eggs are hatched.

- In a bad mood, the Octopus can even bite you or someone from your family.

- The Octopus will spend most of its time hiding in the hiding structures that you provide him. If you have kids in your household, they might get bored with this pet very soon.

- An Octopus is an unusual pet. It will not give you the pleasure of hugging it and playing with it. If you are looking for a pet with whom you can share physical closeness, then the Octopus is not for you.

- Also, with a baby at home, you might not be able to give your pet the attention that it requires.

- If you are fond of pets that love to cuddle, then you should know that Octopuses are not meant for this. You can't hug and cuddle an animal that lives in the water.

- The pet has a lifespan of 4-5 years. This can be a big disadvantage for many people. While you invest a lot of money and emotions on the pet, you will not be able to enjoy the emotional bond for a very long time.

- These animals rest a lot. Though this can be an advantage for you, if you want a pet that will play with you all day, then you are in for a loss.

- The animal can gain weight very easily. They are huge and bulky.

- A lot of care has to be taken to ensure that they maintain good health. They catch disease causing bacteria and viruses very easily. Once infected, it is difficult to treat them.

- The animal can seek a lot of attention. Though the pet is solitary in its nature, there can be phases when he will require you to pamper him a lot.

- The pet can get stressed and depressed very easily. The pet is a defensive pet. He will get scared and stressed, but will not attack. This can affect him a lot.

- If spending too much money is an issue with you, then you will have to think twice before purchasing the animal.

- You should also understand the various other costs that you will encounter while raising your pet. You might have to spend a lot of money on their health.

9. Estimate of cost for domesticating an Octopus

Domesticating an animal is not child's play. While you have to be available emotionally and physically, you also need to provide financial support.

As a prospective owner, you might be wondering about the costs that you need to prepare for when buying and then bringing up an Octopus. You will have many doubts in your head.

As the owner and parent of the pet, you will have to make attempts to fulfil all the needs of the animal. You should also be prepared on the financial front to take care of these needs.

It is better that you plan these things well in advance. This planning will help you to avoid any kind of disappointment that you might face when there are some payments that need to be made.

To clear the various doubts in your head, you should understand the nature of the pet and also the various costs that you will incur while raising the pet.

Your pet Octopus will have various things that will make him different from other pets. There will be specific requirements of the pet. For example, in regards to diet and housing, the animal has some very specific needs.

You should be able to understand the needs and then also fulfil them. This section will help you in understanding what you can expect in terms of finances when you are planning to bring an Octopus into your household.

To begin with, you need money to buy the Octopus. Once you have spent money on buying the animal, you should be ready to spend money on his domestication. You can expect to spend money on the shelter, healthcare and food of the animal.

While there are certain purchases that are only one time and fixed, you will also have to be prepared for unexpected purchases that you will have to face once in a while. You have to be ready to bear various other regular things continuously over the years.

Being well prepared is the best way to go about things. There are basically two kinds of costs that you will be looking to incur, which are as follows:

The one-time or initial costs: The initial costs are the ones that you will have to bear in the very beginning of the process of domestication of the animal. This will include the one-time payment that you will give to buy the animal.

The regular or monthly costs: Even when you are done with the one-time payments, there are some other things that you won't be able to avoid. But, these finances can be planned well in advance. You can maintain a journal to keep track of them.

The monthly costs are the ones that you will have to spend each month or once in few months to raise the Octopus. This category includes the costs of the food requirements and health requirements of the pet.

The various regular veterinarian visits, the sudden veterinarian visits and replacement of things come under the monthly category.

The various purchases you can expect

While you are all excited to domesticate the Octopus, you should also start planning for all that you can expect in the future while raising the pet animal. You can expect to incur the following:

Cost of buying the Octopus

The initial cost of purchasing the Octopus could be higher when compared with the initial cost incurred in purchasing other regular animals. If money is an issue with you, then you will have to think twice before purchasing this animal.

On the other hand, if spending money is not an issue then you should understand the other important factors for raising an Octopus and accordingly make a decision.

You can expect to spend $20/£16.87 to $1000/£843.97 to purchase your Octopus. The price will depend on the colour, age and the health of the animal.

You should make sure that you get the Octopus examined medically before buying it. The examination and tests will also add on to the initial price.

Cost of shelter

When you bring a pet home, you have to make the necessary arrangements to give it a comfortable home. The shelter of the animal will be his home, so it is important that you construct the shelter according to the animal's needs.

The Octopus will require a good quality water tank or aquarium. If their shelter is not comfortable, the pet will be restless all the time. Even if you construct a very basic aquarium for the animal, it should have the necessary comfort.

This is a one-time cost, so you should not try to save money at the cost of the pet's comfort. The cost of shelter will depend on the type of the shelter. You can expect to spend anywhere between $200/£168.73 to $1000/£843.97 for the aquarium of the Octopus. A seventy gallon glass aquarium can be bought at $300/£253.10.

The aquarium should be cycled well. It should also be accessorized well by you. The cage will require some basic stuff, such as live rocks, tunnels and toys.

These are the extra costs that you will have to incur in addition to the cost of the cage. This should cost you around $200/£168.73.

Heat and light source

It is important to maintain the right temperature and light cycle in a octopus's aquarium. If this is not done, the pet can get stressed.

You should just make sure that consistent warm temperature is maintained in the water tank. The pet can get sick and unwell if you fail to maintain the right temperature and light cycle.

Depending on the type and brand of the heat and light sources, you can expect to spend $30/£22.20 to $60/£44.39.

Accessories and hiding place

As an important accessory for the pet's cage, you will have to invest in good quality tunnels. You also need to buy a hiding place for the Octopus.

Cheap plastic materials that can have an adverse effect on the health of the Octopus must be avoided. Similarly, toys that can be shredded or broken should also be avoided.

You also need to provide an igloo-like structure for your pet to hide in. This will make him feel secure. You can prepare one at home with an old plastic tub.

Depending on your choice of toys and hiding place, you can expect to spend about $50/£36.99 to $250/£184.97.

Food

The most important factor that will affect your monthly costs is the food of the pet octopus. The type of the food and the quality of the food that you give to your pet will make an impact on your monthly expenditure on the pet.

A domesticated Octopus will mostly be fed good quality sea food. You might also have to include various supplements to give your pet overall nourishment.

This is important because if the animal does not get all the appropriate nutrients in the right amount, his health will suffer, which again will be an extra cost for you. So, make sure that you provide all the necessary nutrients to your pet animal.

The kinds of food that you feed your pet will also affect the exact food cost that you encounter per month. You should remember that the more lax you are regarding the money that goes into food costs, the lesser would be the amount of money that would go into health care.

If your pet is well fed, it will not fall sick that often. This will automatically reduce the amount of money that you would have to spend on the veterinarian and medication.

You will have some options when it comes to feeding your Octopus. You can choose amongst those options, depending on the availability of the items in your region and also the price of the food items.

You can expect to spend about $75/£63.28 to $300/£253.10 every month on the food of the Octopus.

Cost of health care

It is important to invest in the health of a pet animal. This is necessary because an unhealthy animal is the breeding ground for many other diseases in the home. Your pet might pass on the diseases to other pets if not treated on time. This means danger for the pets and also the members of the family.

You will have to take the Octopus to the veterinarian for regular visits for his health. He will be able to guide you regarding any medications that the pet may need.

It is advised that for the very first year of domestication, you are extra careful regarding the health of the animal.

You should also be prepared for unexpected costs, such as sudden illness or accident of the Octopus. Health care is provided at different costs in different areas. So, the veterinarian in your area could be costlier than the veterinarian in the nearby town.

You should work out all these costs right in the beginning, so that you don't suffer any problems later. Realizing that you can't keep the animal and giving it up is never a good idea.

You should understand that taking care of these animals will require special skills. You should make sure that the veterinarian that you consult for your pet octopus is experienced in handling marine animals.

You should also be prepared to spend more money on their health than what you would have spent on other pet animals. It is believed that you should have an extra $1000/£843.97 saved for your Octopus's emergencies. He might require an operation or surgery because of a disease.

Other costs

Although the main costs that you will encounter while raising your pet have already been discussed, there will be some extra costs that you will have to take care of. Most of these costs are one-time costs.

You will have to spend money to buy stuff such as live rocks for the pet. You can expect to spend $100/£73.99 to $250/£184.97 on these costs. The cost will depend on the wear and tear and the quality of the products.

In order to keep track of the costs that could be awaiting you, you should regularly check the various items in the tank of the pet. If you think that something needs to be repaired or replaced, you should go ahead and do it.

10. Which Octopus should you avoid?

While you are thinking over which species is the most suitable for your household, you should also make an attempt to understand which Octopus you need to avoid. You should avoid keeping a blue ring Octopus.

The blue ring Octopus is generally available for sale in many places. But, this does not mean that this Octopus is ideal for a household. A blue ring Octopus will cost you only around $30/£22.20. It is also known that thousands of these Octopuses are imported in to Europe and United States each year.

There are various reasons why you should avoid keeping a blue ring Octopus. Firstly, the animal has a very short life span. This particular Octopus can live only for a few weeks, so even $30/£22.20 is not actually a great deal.

Secondly, many of these Octopuses die during the shipment process.

11. Giant Pacific Octopus

One of the most common species that is domesticated is the Giant Pacific Octopus (GPO). It is important to understand this particular species of Octopus well if you wish to understand the Octopus in general.

Enteroctopus dofleini, the Giant Pacific Octopus (GPO) is a member of the cephalopod molluscs, an ancient group of highly evolved, active and intelligent predators. Cephalopods mean 'head-foot'. They possess the distinguishing characteristics of a complex nervous system, eggs that generally hatch into miniatures of the adult form (no larval stage) and eight tentacles or arms surrounding the mouth.

This group includes the Octopus, squid, cuttlefish and nautilus. The GPO is the largest of all the Octopus species, normally between 3 and 4 metres and ranging from 20 to 40 kilos. The largest recorded GPO was 71 kg.

Anecdotal reports of a Giant Pacific Octopus with an arms pan of 9 metres have been given. This red colour helps GPO's avoid detection in the murky low light levels they inhabit. These amazing creatures depend on stealth and camouflage to avoid predation and are able to change their colour, pattern and texture to perfectly blend in with their environment and to display to other Octopuses.

Many people believe that Octopus emotions are portrayed by the colour they display, however this is difficult to prove. The arrays of GPO colour and texture in relation to camouflage are currently being investigated at Brighton Sealife Centre, UK.

The Octopus has highly developed senses that enable many of the extraordinary abilities characteristic to these creatures. Each of the 8 arms, in four pairs, possess up to 280 individual suction cups distributed in two rows, these contain thousands of chemical receptors used for taste and smell along with areas around the outer edge of the suckers that are sensitive to touch.

The suction cups are also able to rotate and move independently of the other suckers. These abilities allow the Octopus to distinguish between objects through touch alone, a skill particularly utilised when groping for prey in small dark spaces. In addition to this, they also have the most developed eyes and visual ability of all the invertebrates.

The Octopus generally moves about by crawling, using its arms, but it can move more rapidly by torpedoing along, jetting water through the siphon. When doing this to escape a threat, a cloud of purple black ink may also be released to confuse a potential predator.

This ink can be concentrated or watery dependent on the amount produced and can be projected out of water at unsuspecting aquarists. In aquaria, inking is very unusual and fortunately ink in the water is not toxic to animals.

Octopus can be found foraging at night in the shallower intertidal zone and have even been known to climb right out of the water and pull themselves across rocks to reach tidal pools. Out of the water the mantle cavity holds water enabling the gills to continue extracting oxygen until the water is depleted of oxygen.

After this, the animal is effectively holding its breath. The animal displays a very terrestrial behaviour. But, it is often said that this behaviour is not observed in daylight. If it is captivated, it will try to make its way back to the ocean.

The Octopus is a very stern predator. It is also believed that it is great in grabbing opportunities. It seeks for opportunities during the dusk and the dawn time. The Octopus eats a number of organisms. It can eat crabs and lobsters.

It can also survive bivalve molluscs such as mussels and clams, snails, fish, cat sharks and other Octopus. Using the web-like net between their 8 arms, Octopuses are able to parachute down onto a crab, and tucking in the edges it cuts off all escape routes.

Its hundreds of suction cups on the legs are used to feel and taste for the crab and then when discovered, to pin it down and bring it to the beak. A variety of techniques are employed by the Octopus to enable access to the flesh inside their mostly hard shelled prey. Brute force is often used to rip or bite open the shell.

The keratin beak can bite a hole through the joints of a crustacean's shell and when opening bivalves a rasp like radula can also be used to drill a hole through the shell. Saliva containing a potent neurotoxin called cephalotoxin and digestive enzymes is then injected to swiftly kill the prey within a few seconds of being bitten.

The enzymes are so effective that all the connective tissue and thinner parts of the shell are dissolved in approximately 20 minutes for an average sized shore crab. After the digested crab is sucked out only the carapace and stronger sections of the claws and legs remain to be discarded.

The diversity of prey species can be observed at the entrance to the Octopuses' lair, where the discarded remains of the shells and bones of previously consumed prey are deposited, known as the midden.

Acclimation

When acclimatising Giant Pacific Octopuses, there is little evidence that acclimation needs to be overly protracted. Spending 30 minutes or so mixing the tank water with the bag water using a jug is fine in my experience.

Often after a 25 hour journey it is more important to get them out of the high levels of ammonia they are swimming in than it is to worry about slight stresses caused by changes in salinity, pH or temperature.

In 10 years of doing this I have never had any problems and all the Octopus feed well straight away on arrival. Some other curators disagree and recommend a slower acclimation – Chris Brown at Weymouth Sealife DDD recommends 1.5 - 2 hours to avoid stress of changing pH.

Chapter 3: Owning an Octopus

While you might be extremely upbeat about bringing an invertebrate home, it is necessary that you fully understand the pros and cons of bringing the animal home. Even if you bring a dog home, you have to make sure that you are all ready for the responsibilities ahead. The dog is an easy to keep animal; still its maintenance requires certain efforts from you.

A pet is like a family member. You have to make sure that the animal is taken care of. The animal should be loved in your household. If your family is not welcoming enough for the pet, the animal will lose its sense of being very quickly.

You will see a decline not just in its behaviour but also its health. You should be able to provide the pet a safe and sound home. This is the basic requirement when planning to bring an animal home.

If an easily domesticated animal requires so much efforts and attention on the part of the owner, then imagine how much effort an invertebrate would want? This is not to scare you, but to make you understand that you have to know the right ways to domesticate an invertebrate.

Most often than not people make the mistake of bringing an animal home without realizing its effect on one's life. When you raise a pet, your life and your family's life will also be equally affected. You can't escape that.

It is better to accept this fact and be prepared for it. The last thing that you want is to ditch the animal mid-way realizing that you can't keep it. You should also make sure that your family is comfortable with the pet.

An Octopus is not a very easy animal to keep. It is not a very common pet. This makes it very difficult for people who are interested in keeping the animal. There is a certain life style that the animal is accustomed to. You should be able to give the animal a space that does not disturb its normal lifestyle.

Getting acquainted with marine life by reading more about it is the only way. You should gain experience by keeping relatively easier to keep marine animals. If you have no experience in this field then you will be relieved to learn that many first timers have done well.

But, you should always refrain from buying Octopuses as an impulse reaction. Just because you developed an interest in Octopuses does not mean that you should go and buy four or five of them. This will only lead to confusion on your end. This will also risk the life of these beautiful animals.

It is often advised to domesticate some hardy fish before you go on to keep an Octopus. This will prepare you for the bigger decision of keep an Octopus. You will get better in terms of preparation and also confidence.

You need to give yourself three months for setting up the aquarium and making it ready for the Octopus. If you are planning to setup an aquarium and buy an Octopus at the same time, then you will only be making a mistake.

1. Why should you be so prepared when planning to bring an invertebrate home?

An Octopus is unlike most other pet animals. It requires effort from your side if you wish to keep the animal. It should be noted that because information about the animal as a pet is not too vast, there are many doubts in the mind of people.

Many of you might wonder as to what is so special about bringing an Octopus home. Why isn't it like getting any other pet? To clear this doubt and many other similar doubts, the following list has been created:

In regards to diet and housing, the Octopus has some very specific needs. You should be able to understand the needs and then also fulfil them.

The animal is not a regular pet that is found in many homes. You will have to understand the ways to deal with different things related to the animal.

Such animals are different in their demeanour. Though the Octopuses are known to be very friendly and affectionate, it will have certain traits that might differ from your usually domesticated animals.

If you are expecting your Octopus to behave like your cat or your dog, then you should better get the dog and the cat. You should understand that the Octopus, even after being domesticated, will have its own unique ways. It is important to let the animal be. You should not try to change the basic demeanour of the Octopus in a bid to hand raise it.

Bringing an aquatic animal home is a huge responsibility. You should be well prepared for it. There is no use crying later. All aquatic animals pose a challenge when you try to domesticate them. An Octopus is all the more difficult to keep if you don't understand its requirements very clearly and precisely.

If the pet Octopus gets sick, you should know what to do. It is important that you are not clueless and tensed in such a situation. Only a person who is well prepared will be able to take the responsibility of the animal's good health.

Anything that is not understood is very difficult. Once you understand the dos and don'ts of raising the Octopus in your home, you will realize that it is not that difficult. All you need to do is understand the right ways to do the right things.

This chapter and the subsequent chapters will help you to prepare yourself for domesticating the Octopus. You will be able to understand whether domesticating an Octopus is something for you or not. It will also help you to go forward in the right direction while caring for your Octopus.

2. The right number

If you are looking at getting more than one Octopus or other aquatic animals along with the Octopus, then the most obvious concern that you might have is whether this is easy. It is important that each animal in the household is compatible with each other; else there would be too much chaos and trouble, not just for the animals but also for you.

How difficult is it to domesticate more than one invertebrate at a time? How many should I buy? What is the right number? Would the invertebrates compete with each other for the basic necessities and the luxuries they are provided with? Would they be friendly with each other? These are the most obvious questions that would be running in the head of a person looking to buy more than one invertebrate.

If you are looking at getting more than one invertebrate, then you should understand the right decision would depend of a number of factors. It will depend on the following few factors:

- Space

- Personality of the invertebrates

- Size considerations

- Gender considerations

When looking to domesticate more than one invertebrate, then one of the most important criteria that need to be kept in mind is the space that you would provide the invertebrates. These animals are known to be very active. You should be able to provide them a space where they can move around without any constraints.

The important point that needs to be understood here is that domestication of even a single Octopus will require ample space. The Octopus will grow at a very fast pace. They need space to roam around and also to hide.

You should also understand that as the Octopus and other invertebrates grow, they need more space. If you plan on keeping more than one Octopus, or if you want to keep other invertebrates along with the Octopus, then you would have to give them more space when they grow.

It is important that the tank or the aquarium is big enough to house all the animals. The animals shouldn't have to compete amongst themselves for space. If they have to do so, it will affect their overall growth in a very negative way.

The lesser the space for the invertebrates, the more difficult it will get for you to raise your pets. So, space is one factor that will always be important when you are hand raising your Octopus or Octopuses.

If there is one factor that drastically affects the number of invertebrates that can be kept together, then it is the space that you have.

- Octopus and other invertebrates are very active in nature. They will always be on the move, so it is important to give them a good amount of space.

- If the space, which is the tank or the aquarium you would provide the pets is very limited, then you need to think about your decision to get more than one invertebrate.

- The Octopus and the other invertebrates get tense, stressed and unhealthy if they are not given enough space to themselves.

- It has been seen in the past that when Octopuses and other aquatic animals are kept in closed quarters within a small tank, they tend to become unhealthy and unfit. In such cases, they don't serve as ideal animals for domestication.

3. Are you prepared to domesticate an Octopus?

You can't domesticate an animal only because the animal looks good. If this is the only reason that motivates you to bring animal such as an Octopus home, then it is time that you rethink about your idea to domesticate the animal.

Octopuses are not very easy to keep. They require your patience, understanding, determination, time and money. If you don't have these things to offer to your pet Octopus, then you will not be able to raise the pet well.

If you are contemplating on the idea to bring the pet home, then it is important that you know whether you are ready or not.

- Do you have the time to take care of the pet? Do you have the patience that is required to domesticate this invertebrate?

- Do you meet all the legal requirements for domesticating the pet? Is it even legal to domesticate them in your area? You might also need a permit to take it from one state to another. You should make sure that you understand all the legal formalities before you buy a pet. Different animals have different legal regulations. It is important to understand these regulations before you bring a pet animal home.

- Are you prepared for the long term commitment of raising the animal? Do you have the means and the money for it? Raising a pet animal at home is always a long term commitment. It will require your patience and hard work along with financial commitment.

- Octopuses are known to be very intelligent and fast. You will have to be prepared for various surprises that the Octopus will have for you. Do you have that kind of energy for them?

- These animals will hide a lot in their hiding places. You need to be prepared for this.

- These animals can be very unpredictable. They can be very moody. Do you have the patience to deal with such behaviour?

- A small area is not enough for the overall development of the Octopus. The Octopus needs enough space to move around in the tank. Can you provide that kind of space in your home?

- Octopuses can be very mischievous. If you wish to bring them home, you should be prepared for this.

- There are certain specific requirements that come along with each pet. For example, your Octopus needs enough space in the water tank to roam around and also hide. They need to let them be if you want them to be happy.

- They have to roam around and exercise themselves. This makes it important for an adult to be around the pet at all times. Can you make sure that such adult supervision can be provided at your home?

- Do you have a kid under the age of 5 years at your home? Or are you planning to have a baby soon? If yes, then it might not be a good idea to buy the pet. This is because kids under the age of 5 years should not be allowed to be near the pet because of their unpredictable behaviour.

- Also, with a baby at home, you might not be able to give your pet the attention that it requires.

- If you are fond of pets that love to cuddle, then you should know that Octopuses are not meant for this. You can't hug and cuddle an animal that lives in the water.

- If you take them in your arms to cuddle them, they will just play and enjoy themselves.

To ensure that your Octopus lives a happy and healthy life at your home, it is more than important that you prepare yourself in the best possible way.

You should make sure that you evaluate your resources well. It is also important to understand if your family is ready to domesticate the Octopus or not. It might look like an overwhelming task, but it is important because bringing a new life home is a matter of great responsibility.

4. Ensuring your Safety

If you are domesticating a Giant Pacific Octopus, you should be very careful. There are a few things that you need to take care of. Don't bring your arm near to the beak of the Octopus. It should be noted that a bite from a Giant Pacific Octopus is very painful. It can be very serious also. The Neurotoxin the GPO uses to kill crabs is in the saliva and a bite, although rare, could be dangerous to humans.

Enzymes in the saliva are used to digest the flesh of crustacean prey and this can cause a necrotic wound that does not heal and swells badly. To date, no fatalities have been recorded from GPO bites, but bites must be avoided, and a bite requires urgent medical attention. The application of heat is recommended to counter the effects of the neurotoxin and enzymes. Aquarists need to be fully trained before working with this species.

To begin with it is good practice to only allow arm tips to stick onto you and to ensure one hand is always free so that you can safely remove the Octopus if you want to. At Blue Reef we have a rule that you should only have a maximum of 3 arms holding onto you at any one time. As you become more relaxed and you get to know your Octopus you can let them put more arms on you.

Even small Octopuses are capable of pulling you very hard when they want to. Suction cups are capable of producing 'love bites' on the skin, although they soon fade and humans don't have any adverse reactions to contact. If you want a Giant Pacific Octopus to let go of you, simply squeeze its arm firmly – they don't like it and will always let go quickly.

Be careful not to dig into the flesh with your nails. It seems to be very difficult to injure the arm of an Octopus but obviously don't squeeze it so hard that the arm is damaged, stay calm and gradually apply pressure until the animal stops holding on.

They soon learn that you are not food and you rarely need to squeeze them hard more than a few times before they know not to mess with you. It has been observed at Blue Reef Newquay that a Giant Pacific Octopus will recoil if touched by warm dry hands – and will often let go of the keeper – this is risky if a member of the public touches the Octopus while a keeper is holding the animal out of the water as it may fall out of the tank so our policy is not to let people touch the Octopus without wet hands.

It is also important to wash hands carefully before interacting with the Octopus to remove soaps and hand creams that may harm the Octopus. They do love the taste of fish on your skin though. Despite all these factors, overall the risks involved with Octopus enrichment are relatively easy to control and the benefits of regular enrichment and play out-weigh these risks.

5. Precautions to be Taken

You should understand that there are certain precautions that each owner should follow when domesticating an Octopus. It is very important that you get acquainted with the dos and don'ts of keeping the animal.

You have to allow yourself the time to understand the behaviour, mannerisms, habits and moods of the pet. This will allow you avoid unpleasant incidents for your pet Octopus.

This will help you and your family to be safe. And, this will also allow the pet octopus to be secure at all times.

Precautions at Home

There are many precautions that you would be required to observe at your home. These precautions will make sure that the invertebrate is safe and secure. These precautions will also help you and your family to avoid any danger or injury. It is important everybody in the family is safe and sound.

Nobody should hurt the Octopus, and nobody should be injured by him. By nature, the Octopus is very unpredictable. If taken care of in an appropriate manner, the animal can be very friendly, but still the basic nature of the animal can't be changed.

There are a few precautions that you should follow when looking after the pet at home. These precautions will depend on the conditions of your household, whether you have children or not and whether you have other pets or not. The various scenarios and how you should take care of your pet octopus have been discussed in this section.

Precautions with Children

If you have children at home, then you need to train your children before expecting the pet to behave in a certain way and manner. The children need to be taught about the unpredictable nature of the pet. The children should understand that the pet is different from usual pets.

The children should understand the basic nature of the Octopus. It is also important that they are taught what to expect and what not to expect. The children can't have unreal expectations that the Octopus will start running around the house with them.

The children should be taught how to behave responsibly around the water tank. They should not put hazardous things in the tank. Teaching the kids such things is also a great learning experience for the children. They should never to be allowed to do something nasty.

You should keep children below the age of five away from the pet. The simple reason for this is that smaller kids will not understand how to behave with the pet. The kids of this age will not know the limits that they shouldn't cross with the pet. This will mean that both the kids and pet will become a danger for each other.

The kids below the age of five will not be able to understand the specific requirements and also reactions of the pet. Even if they are under adult supervision, there are high chances of a mishap. So, in the best interest of the pet and also the child, you should keep smaller kids away from the water tank containing the Octopus.

You should make sure that the older children are around the pet only under your supervision or some adult supervision. If your kid is older, you can allow him to be around the water tank with the pet. But, you should make sure that the child understands the actions and reactions of the pet well.

You should have a discussion with the kid as to how the Octopus is different from the rest of the pets. It is important that the kid knows the pet well. You should also make sure that you don't scare your child away. You need to inform him for his own safety.

But, that does not mean that he should be scared of his pet. When the kid understands how he should behave with the pet animal, he makes it easier for himself to have a great bond with the animal.

Precautions with other pets of the house

Since the Octopus is in a water tank, he doesn't have much to do with other pets. An Octopus might not be too good with other marine animals, such as fish. There have been instances where the Octopus has eaten up the fish.

If the animal does not sense any potential danger from the other animal, he will be cordial with it. The octopus might not be very cordial with animals that are smaller in size than him.

By nature, an Octopus sees an animal smaller than his size as a food item for him. He will have his tendency to harm this smaller pet and make it its prey. If you have very small fish, you should keep them away from the Octopus.

The octopus can have his own preferences. For example, the pet Octopus might like a certain kind of fish more than the other. The fish will also not feel very comfortable around the pet because of its high energy levels. But, the pet might not be very fond of some kinds of marine animals.

In particular, an Octopus will be fond of pets that it grew up with. The Octopus will also be fine with pets larger in size than him. If you want to have more pets in the household, make sure that they are brought around the same time and are in the similar age range. This will help them to bond well.

When you first introduce your pets to each other, you need to be extra cautious. In the beginning, keep the pets away from each other, but in the same vicinity so that they can identify with each other's smell.

If you have pets that are smaller in size compared to your Octopus, then you should keep the pets away from the Octopus. For example, if you have a small turtle, rabbit, bird or a rodent in the house, they need to be away from the Octopus for their own safety. Your Octopus might attack the smaller pet and might try to eat it, if you are not careful enough to keep them away.

It is important to note that even if the pets in the household seem friendly and cordial to each other, you should make sure that there is some supervision when they are together. You never know when they get hostile towards each other for some petty issue.

Chapter 4: Reproduction

As a new owner of a cephalopod, you might be interested in the reproduction cycle and procedure of the Octopus. The reproduction in Octopuses is known to be very challenging. But, it will get easier to understand once you equip yourself with all the right knowledge. This chapter is meant to clear all your doubts regarding the reproduction in Octopuses.

You should know that breeding in Octopuses is defined as the production of an offspring by mating of the Octopuses. It is important to understand the breeding patterns of your pet animals. How well you understand the mating patterns of your pet will also determine how well you look after the pet.

Keeping and caring for an animal in your home also means that you understand each aspect of their lives. Reproduction is an important aspect of any animal's life. This is the way the species can continue to survive.

You can't and shouldn't ignore such an important aspect of the Octopus's life. You should also understand the effect of reproduction on the life of the Octopus. This will allow you to understand the life of the cephalopod in greater depth.

When you are conducting controlled mating at your home, there are many things that you will have to take care of. You should make sure that the male and the female Octopus are ready for mating. They should have reached the right maturity level.

After they have mated, you should be ready to take care of the female and the eggs. It is also important that you take care of the nesting requirements of the Octopuses once the mating is over and the female pet Octopus is pregnant.

1. Basic information regarding breeding

When you get an Octopus home, it is very important to understand its breeding cycle. Each animal species has their unique breeding habits and patterns. When you are looking to take care of your pet well, you should also lay enough emphasis on understanding his breeding patterns.

For certain species of the Octopus, there are many rituals attached to mating. On the other hand, there are a few species that go about mating in a very subdued manner. There is nothing exciting about the entire process.

An Octopus will have the inner urges or desires to indulge in mating once it grows up. This is natural in all species. It is important to understand the effect of reproduction or mating on Octopuses.

Both the male and female Octopus dies after mating, but the duration of their lives after mating differs. It is known that a male Octopus will not be able to survive for more a few months after it has mated with a female Octopus.

A female Octopus also can't make it too far after it has mated with the male Octopus. It is said that a female Octopus will die after the eggs that it laid have hatched.

You should understand the natural mating behavior of your pet animals. This will help you to do the right thing when breeding them. This chapter is meant to equip you with all the knowledge that you might need for mating your Octopuses.

It should be noted that an Octopus has two main ways to reproduce. These can be called his main strategies. A common Octopus is capable of laying many eggs at a time. It can lay over 200000 eggs. There are many other species that can lay over 500 eggs. This will help you to understand which Octopus is easy to rear and which is not.

A good breeder will always encourage you to thoroughly understand the sexual tendencies of your Octopuses so as to not commit any mistake in the future. You need to know how often and in what conditions your Octopuses can reproduce.

In the wild, the baby Octopuses have a higher chances of survival in a warm environment. This means that the Octopuses enter their mating cycle in the right temperatures. You can expect the same when the Octopuses are domesticated.

When an Octopus is in its natural environment, the extra amount of light during the summers and also spring brings about a change in its body. The male and female Octopus gets sexually active during this time.

A male Octopus will display changes in his behavior. He will seem more aggressive and restless. This is due to the sex hormones that have become active in his body. This is how you can identify if your male pet animal is ready to mate or not.

2. Mating and birthing process of the Octopuses

The breeding of Octopuses is often said to be challenging. The reason behind this is that because these animals were earlier not domesticated and are still widely found in the wild. This makes it difficult for people to observe and then understand their breeding and mating routines.

Even after the domestication of cephalopods started, there are many species of Octopus and other cephalopods that are not domesticated. Not much is known about the domestication of such species.

You should understand the following points to understand the mating and the birthing process of the Octopus.

It is known that the male Octopus plays an active part in the mating process. In fact, the female counterpart does not have much of a role to play.

The females remain extremely timid and passive during the entire process of mating.

The male Octopus is known to be focussed and concentrated towards the act from the start to the end. The female will have conceived by the end of the mating process.

It is said that after the female conceives, she goes into a phase of gestation. The gestation period, or phase, typically has a duration of 30 to 38 days.

If the female Octopus is observed after her gestation period, you will come to know when she will give birth to another Octopus.

For a few hours before the birthing takes place, the female Octopus starts cleaning its pouch. This could be an indication that she is all ready to welcome the infant into her life and pouch.

She will be seen cleaning her abdominal area. In fact, the female spends many hours in this cleaning process. She will lick her abdominal area and make a trail from there up to the stomach.

Once the contractions begin, the female Octopus can be seen looking for a vertical object for support. In the wild, she would look for a wood log or a tree. If someone is around during the contraction phase of the female Octopus, it is always good to keep something that the female can use in her vicinity.

This phase will go on for a long time. The female Octopus will experience contractions every now and then. This will difficult for her, but this is the only way to bring the new life into form.

After this, the female will get ready to give birth to an infant, who will depend on her for a long time for all his needs.

The small and wriggling infant will be born soon. It should be noted that when the infant is born, he is still attached to the mother physically.

After giving birth to the baby Octopus, the mother will move and come in a sitting position. This is to aid the baby Octopus to reach the mother Octopus.

Soon after the mother sits, the infant can be seen floating and climbing towards the pouch of his mother Octopus. In almost ten minutes, the baby is able to get inside. After reaching, the baby Octopus makes sure that it immediately attaches its body to the teat of his mother.

It should be noted that the infant would remain in this position where it is attached to the teat for about 4 to 6 months. The precise duration of this process depends on a number of factors, such as the species and the sub species.

The various species have their own specific duration of attaching and remaining in the pouch. No matter which species is in consideration, the infant will come out in a few weeks.

A pet is like a family member. You will be more like a parent than like a master to the pet. You will be amazed to see how much love and affection your Octopus will give through his ways and actions.

But, for that to happen, you have to make sure that the animal is taken care of. The animal should be loved in your household. If your family is not welcoming enough for the pet, the animal will lose its sense of being very quickly.

The diet of the Octopus will have a direct effect on the way he feels and functions. As the owner of the pet, it will be your responsibility that the pet is fed the right food in the right amounts and at the right times.

You will also have to make sure that the pet is safe and secure at all times. It is important that you learn about the common health issues that the Octopus is likely to suffer from. This will help you to avoid these health conditions and keep the Octopus safe.

It should be noted that an Octopus has no fat reserve. The Octopus can convert muscle to energy. During senescence, the body weight drops to almost half.

3. Understanding a young Octopus

It should be noted here that a young Octopus is capable of growing up very fast. An Octopus has a life span of a very few years. It shows rapid growth right from the very beginning.

A juvenile Octopus can rapidly increase its body size. The food that you serve the Octopus will be utilized properly by the body of the animal.

It is estimated that an Octopus, even the young one, is capable of increasing the mass of its body by over five per cent every single day. In fact, after the Octopus dies, it weighs almost one third of the weight of all the food that it had eaten in its life.

When you bring a pet home, it is more like a new member of the family. It is very important that you take time to understand the various stages in the pet's life, as each stage will demand different care and methods.

In case you decide to breed your Octopus, you will face the situation where you will have to take care of a young one. There are many people who buy young Octopuses from the breeders and also have to face the same situation.

Hand rearing a baby animal can be very tricky, but if you pay attention to the details, it will be fun and interesting. You should take care of a few things to make sure that your baby Octopus is taken care of.

If, for some reason, a mother is not capable of taking care of the young, then the babies can be given to another female that is in the same age group as the mother. This should be done in the first few days of kindling, preferably the first three to four days.

It should also be noted that body temperature regulation is very important for a young pet, but a baby animal is unable to regulate the temperature of his body. You will have to make sure that the baby Octopus is experiencing the right temperatures.

He has to be warm at all times, but make sure that the temperature does not get too hot, as this can also be harmful for the Octopus. You will have to constantly monitor the temperature so that it does not overheat the infant.

4. Raising a baby Octopus

You need to be well prepared when you have to hand rear an infant. It can be very challenging if you don't get your basics right. While you might have learnt it all, there are a few important points that need to be remembered when taking care of the infant Octopus.

To hand rear the infant Octopus, you will need to follow the following points:

There is a simple formula for the feed that you should be giving your infant. You should make sure that the water you use to prepare the formula has been cooled after heating it.

It should also be noted that body temperature regulation is very important for a young pet, but a baby animal is unable to regulate the temperature of his body.

It should be noted that you should not use cold water because it is not right for the formula. You should also not use boiling water because it can again destroy the mineral content of the formula.

A simple way to make use of the water is to boil the water, and then let the boiled water cool down. This information can be used to plan the further activities.

Chapter 5: Setting up the tank

Domesticating an Octopus requires a lot of planning. You can't buy one from the store and domesticate it without a proper plan because that won't work for you.

It is always advised to read more and more about the subject to get yourself acquainted and fully prepared. It is also suggested to start with other marine life. This will give you some experience.

Keeping an aquatic animal is a different challenge as compared to keeping a land animal. There is no denying this fact. To make things smoother for you, it is a better idea to start with animals that are easier to keep.

For example, you can keep fish to get acquainted with marine life. It is always a good idea to keep other invertebrates before you can keep Octopus. This will help you gain some insight and experience.

You should also remember that there are no rights and wrongs here. Though it is advised to start with relatively easier invertebrates, this does not mean that you can't keep an Octopus right in the beginning.

There are many people who have managed to keep Octopus without any prior experience of invertebrate life. It completely depends on you and your choice. Just be aware of the pros and cons of both.

In any case you have to make some preparations before you can keep an Octopus. It is suggested to keep three months aside preparing the aquarium for the Octopus in your home.

This chapter will help you with an equipment list that will allow you to prepare the aquarium for the new invertebrate that you will bring to your place. Proper care is of utmost importance for the pet invertebrate.

It is known that many invertebrates lose their lives because of the lax attitude of their owners. If you are not careful, you will only lose your pet Octopus.

If you don't have any experience of keeping a marine animal, then you need to understand this step very well. It is important to understand the cycle of maturing a tank. This is a way of ensuring that your marine animals lead a happy life.

It is very important to make sure that the tank is closed properly because an Octopus will escape from any hole or outlet that he finds. The Octopus can come out of a hole that is as huge as its beak.

There are many ways to make sure that your tank is escape proof. This section will help you to understand those ways.

Improper equipment can kill an animal. If you are a novice when it comes to keeping an Octopus then you need to pay all the more attention to this step. A small error on your part can kill the poor animal.

There are many people that want to keep an Octopus at home. The first question that bothers these people is how they will manage to keep the right environment in the tank. This will require consistent effort from your side, but in turn you will be able to keep your Octopus happy and healthy.

When you go to buy an Octopus, you will be surprised to learn that many of the shops that sell these animals have no knowledge of the species they are selling. These shops will refer to the Octopuses with general names such as 'Bali Octopuses, 'Brown Octopus' and 'Common Octopus'.

You should never buy from these shops. It is better to know the species of the Octopus. This will affect the way you keep the Octopus.

1. Aquarium

The Octopus is a marine invertebrate. You have to arrange for a water tank or an aquarium to the house the invertebrate. This is the first and foremost requirement of the pet.

If you already have a fish aquarium in your home, you can convert the same into a water tank for the Octopus. You would have to take certain precautions for the same.

The marine aquarium should never have been treated with copper. This can make the water toxic for the Octopus. Copper is generally used to treat certain diseases such as ich in fish.

You should also make sure that all the fish are removed from the tank. If you allow the fish to be in the tank, the Octopus will treat them as its food. You would definitely not want this.

If the fish do not become food for the Octopus, they can pester the invertebrate and make things difficult for him.

It is said that when you are installing a water tank or an aquarium in your home, you should work as if you are setting up a mini coral reef tank in the house. The preparation of the two will essentially remain the same.

Size of the aquarium

The first step when you are planning to buy an Octopus is to get an aquarium. And, the first step in preparing an aquarium is to understand the size requirements of the aquarium.

It should be noted that the size of the aquarium directly depends on the size and species of the Octopus. The various species have different requirements.

Octopus bimaculoides, or bimac, is one of the common choices of pet Octopus in the United States of America. This particular Octopus requires a very large aquarium.

It is known that an aquarium of 50 gallon size is considered a minimum for this particular species. The bigger the tank is, the better it is.

The size of Giant Pacific Octopus display is an important consideration – given a suitable quantity of food, Giant Octopuses will rapidly grow to at least 2 meters arm span within 6 months of arrival as a 50cm juvenile.

On a normal diet they should not get much larger than this but it is important that they have space to move around freely and exhibit normal feeding and foraging behaviour.

The triangular shaped GPO tank at Seattle aquarium designed by Dr Roland Anderson has a total volume of 13,638 litres. It is arguable that you could give a GPO too large a display as particularly in males their activity increases prior to senescence as they have a hormonal urge to find females.

Given a very large tank they can potentially injure themselves by crashing into rockwork when jetting backwards. Also, a larger display can mean that the Octopus is further away from customers and is not as visible – potentially negating the purpose of the display.

Quarantine tank facilities

Quarantine tanks for Giant Pacific Octopuses don't need to be quite as large as a display tank as they usually will not hold a full size active adult Octopus. Instead they are more likely to be used to house newly arrived young specimens or senescent adults.

At blue reef Newquay a 2m diameter circular vat is used with sand filtration and a lid made of netting. Weymouth Sealife Displays Development Department have recently installed a large system with 2 square tanks with removable dividers enabling up to 4 Octopuses to be kept in each tank at one time.

Tanks are 2.4m x 2.4m x 1.2m depth (actual water depth 0.8-1M). This provides 4 tanks of 1.2m cubes.

Another consideration is that water should not be mixed between tanks holding senescent Octopuses and younger Octopuses as it has been shown that hormones carried from the senescent Octopus can affect the behaviour of a younger animal.

Display tank design considerations

There are tanks that have a curved and acrylic front. These tanks have many advantages such as deflection of an Octopus that is jetting. They do not stop it in a way that causes damage to the mantle tip. Having easy access to the top of the tank is important to allow easy maintenance – also worth considering is having access from the front of the tank so that aquarists can engage with the public when playing with the Octopus – this makes for a much more exiting and engaging talks when carrying out Octopus enrichment plays and feeds.

It is important to consider the effects of condensation caused by tank water being considerably colder than the surrounding air. Condensation is reduced by using thick acrylic for viewing windows as opposed to less insulating standard glass.

Additionally air flow should be set up blowing dry air onto windows. If you are not able to do this, soap can be used to lather the glass – when the tiny bubbles clear this reduces condensation build up for a short period.

Material of the aquarium

When you go to buy an aquarium or when you plan to install a water tank, you will have to decide on the material of the aquarium or water tank. This is an important decision because this will have a long term effect on the keeping of the animal.

It is suggested that you opt for a glass aquarium or acrylic aquarium. These are the usual aquariums that you will find in most stores that house marine life in water tanks.

Lids

The fact that Octopuses are able to leave water and walk on land was known in Aristotle's time but it was not until the advent of public aquaria that we knew that the Octopus will willingly escape in order to forage for prey.

Many similar reports of Octopuses escaping have been documented over the years since and as a result it is common knowledge that an Octopus aquarium needs a tightly fitting lid! Lids have successfully been constructed out of wood, fibreglass, plastic coated wire and net (always stretched taught across the top of the tank).

GRP grating has been show to contain copper (Horniman Museum, 2010) and may not be suitable for use in tanks although the Deep used this material as a lid for many years. Gaps in lids for pipes etc. can be filled with filter floss which seems to repel the Octopus.

Anderson states that the preferred method of filtration is flow through of natural sea water. This is not always possible and when keeping this species in European aquariums it is rarely possible due to sea water temperatures being outside of the preferred range for much of the year.

Additionally waste water from GPO tanks flowing back into the sea could potentially carry diseases and larvae to the local environment. For this reason, it has until recently been a condition set by CEFAS (Centre for Environment, Fisheries and Aquaculture Science) that any discharged water is treated with caustic soda to kill potential pathogens.

The repeal of this regulation in 2010 has been welcomed by public aquaria as using caustic soda is impractical and as yet there is no evidence that diseases are a problem and no UK aquaria to date are attempting to breed this species in captivity.

Filtration of Octopus tanks can be achieved using many different methods- reverse flow under gravel filtration with a top over flow is the method used at Blue Reef Newquay, and at Blue Reef Portsmouth, this allows the removal of shed skin from suction cups that otherwise build up on the substrate.

Aquarium hood

Octopuses are very popular for their antics. There are some species that are very notorious for escaping. You might keep wondering while your Octopus might have escaped from the tank.

For all those people who are not aware of this, it is important to know that Octopuses can easily escape from water tanks that are not secured well.

It should be noted that different species of Octopuses display different mannerisms. There are some species that are very notorious for their escaping capabilities.

There have been many cases where the Octopus was found dead on the floor. The Octopus will escape from the smallest exit that it will find. In a bid to escape, the Octopus can injure itself and can even die.

You can get an escape proof lid made when you are installing the water tank. A simple way to make your tank safe is to place a cover made of glass between the aquarium hood and the aquarium top.

A simple arrangement like this can go a long way in making sure that the pet Octopus stays where it is supposed to stay. The setting gives him no scope to sneak away from the aquarium.

You will be surprised to know that some species of Octopus can even move the lids that you place over the aquarium. This can be a reason for panic for many people.

A simple way to solve this problem is to make use of heavy lids. These lids become immovable because of their weight. This makes it impossible for the pet Octopus to lift them or move them.

It is also important that all the pipes that run towards or from the filters, air pumps and heaters are meshed well. This will mean that the Octopus will not be able to climb the pipes.

You can also use a sponge with these pipes. The sponge will allow the flow of air but will restrict the movements of the Octopus. This will mean that the Octopus will not be able to climb the pipes.

When you have an Octopus at home, you have to ensure that the pet is safe at all times. The Octopus is so naughty and intelligent that you might be surprised by his antics. This makes it very important that you understand the behaviour of your pet very well.

An Octopus has a very curious personality. He will not think twice before charging into unknown territory. You might be busy with some work, and before you know it your pet Octopus might be walking into some real danger.

You should know that a pet animal like the Octopus has a tendency to injure himself. If you don't pay attention, the damage could be very serious and irrevocable. This is the last thing that you would want for your pet.

A solution to keep your Octopus safe is to proof your water tank. When you set up an aquarium or water tank in your home, lay enough importance to how you will make it escape proof.

An aquarium hood will ensure that the Octopus does not escape from the water tank. This is a simple way to keep yourself tension free. You don't want to worry about the Octopus escaping from the water tank.

Make sure you proof your water tank well and keep your pet away from potential dangers. There is no use to cry after the damage has been done. It is always better to take the necessary precautions in the very beginning.

Your Octopus could actually shock you with the kind of things it can get hurt from. You should make sure any such potentially dangerous things are always out of the reach of the pet Octopus.

Accessories

You should make sure that your Octopus plays with the right kind of toys. Cheap plastic materials that can have an adverse effect on the health of the Octopus must be avoided. Similarly, toys that can be shredded or broken should also be avoided.

The Octopus might accidentally swallow the small or shredded pieces. Make sure that the toys that you allow the pet to play with are of good quality. They should be safe for the Octopus, and they should be impossible to swallow for him. The plastic rolls of toilet paper can be very harmful for the Octopus because he can get his head stuck in it.

You should make sure any such potentially dangerous things are out of the reach of the Octopus. Keep the bin and plastic shells away from him because he might try to play with things that could be harmful for him. This might be very difficult for you in the beginning to look into areas and places that have hidden dangers for the pet.

But, you will definitely learn with time and experience. Things in the aquarium should be pet-friendly. You should make sure there are no sharp edges that could hurt the animal. Also, make sure that the Octopus can't climb on the furniture.

If your pet Octopus swallows something toxic for him, you might not even get a chance to take him to the veterinarian and save him. The digestive system of the animal is such that blockages can happen easily and they can be very dangerous. There are many animals that lose their lives because of such blockages.

This makes it very important to look for areas of hidden dangers and keep the pet safe. The Octopus will try to swallow anything it can. It will try to swallow rubber items, though such things are very harmful for him. It is you who needs to make sure that the pet does not chew on the wrong items.

While they might like chewing on them, these materials when ingested will cause blockage of the digestive tract. You have to take measures to avoid such incidents in your home.

Water sterilization

The use of Ozone in protein skimming has been shown to have a detrimental effect on the health of cephalopods and for this reason it is not recommended to be used for GPO tanks. UV is a suitable alternative for water strerilization but it is not always necessary if frequent water changes are being carried out.

Electrical safety

Regarding electrical safety it is important to remember these Octopuses are able to direct jets of water out of the tank if they feel like it. For this reason electrical sockets and appliances in the area of the tank should be IP rated (preferably water proof) to prevent electric shocks.

Sensitivity to water quality

It should be noted that compared to a fish, an Octopus is much more sensitive to the quality of water. You would require only a few hours or days to prepare the water for a fish.

On the other hand, you need approximately three months if you are looking forward to keeping an Octopus. This time is required to make the water suitable to house the Octopus.

It should be noted that an Octopus will not be able to survive if the water is not of the appropriate quality. Make sure that you allow the water to settle and become suitable for the pet.

The water tank should be cycled for a minimum for three months. This is also known as maturing of the water. When the water is allowed to mature, it becomes fit for the invertebrates.

Water that is cycled well will not have harmful chemicals dissolved in it. The chemicals will settle down during the entire process. The water will allow the growth of useful algae on live rocks.

This, in turn, will also facilitate the growth of the Octopus in the water tank. You have to understand the plight of the poor Octopus also. He is taken away from his natural environment and put in captivity.

The best you can do is to keep the environment around him as close as possible to his natural environment.

Reverse osmosis water

As discussed earlier, the quality of water is very important for the survival of the pet Octopus. It should be noted that the water that is good for human consumption might not be good for the Octopus.

It is important that you get the water tested before you use it for the water tank of the Octopus. You should never use tap water directly for the aquarium. This might be extremely toxic for the pet Octopus.

Even if you get pure drinking water at your home, you can't trust the same for the Octopus. This water has a lot of chemicals in it which are added to make the water pure. This can be very harmful for the pet Octopus.

Water authorities in most areas add fluorine, chlorine and chloramines to make the water fit for consumption. All these salts are known to be unsafe for cephalopods.

Run offs from farms and factories also contain nitrates and phosphates which again are unsafe for Octopuses. Nitrates and phosphates are extremely harmful for most aquatic animals including Octopuses.

Aquarists around the world have tried various ways to make water safe for a pet Octopus. Reverse osmosis unit is one such way to make the water fit for the Octopus and other cephalopods.

A reverse osmosis unit is a special unit that is capable of making the water safe for cephalopods. You can get your home water tested and then invest in such a unit.

There are many aquarium shops that sell reverse osmosis water for people who are interested in keeping cephalopods. This water is sold in barrels. You can look for this in areas around your home. This will make your work easier.

Aquarium salts and salinity of water

You can easily buy synthetic sea salt from any local shop. You can also easily buy it online. Buy this salt and put it in your water tank and aquarium when you are allowing it to mature.

The synthetic salt is made for aquaculture. No matter what kind of salts you use, you will not be able to provide the real seawater. This salt can help you do so. So, it is important to use this salt for the water in the aquarium.

You must be wondering as to how much of this synthetic sea salt needs to be used. There are many people that keep the concentration less than the concentration in seawater.

It should be noted that the salinity of the water is very important for the Octopus. The given composition is suited well for most fish. Fish don't need salinity equal to the seawater.

Carrying out water tests

You would have understood by now that conducting water tests is very important before you can expect to keep an Octopus in your aquarium. These water tests enable you to make your water fit for the Octopus.

As a novice, you might be wondering about various ways to conduct the water tests. It is important that you don't skip these tests. Lack of information can sometimes force people to quit such important steps.

The main aim of a water test in case of domesticating an Octopus is to determine whether the water is fit for the Octopus by checking its salt concentration. This will help you to make the desired changes.

You need a test kit and also a hydrometer to conduct a water test successfully. You can buy a test kit and keep it with you, or you can take rent one. The initial tests can be conducted with the help of LFS.

If you are thinking that only a single water test is required, then you are wrong. It should be noted here that you will have to conduct water tests regularly. This will help you to keep the quality of the water intact.

Ammonia is very toxic for the Octopus. It is also responsible for polluting the water of the water tank. You need to check the levels of ammonia at regular intervals to keep it low.

Apart from checking the levels of ammonia in the water tank, you also need to check for salinity or gravity of water, nitrite and nitrate levels in the water. You also need to check the PH of the water to keep the level optimal.

2. Live rocks

You should also keep a rock named as live rock inside the aquarium. This will help to make the water more suitable for the Octopus and other cephalopods in general.

For those of you who are new to marine life forms, you should know that live rock is a rock that has growth of various life forms on it. The rock could have a growth of algae or sponges.

If you think that this kind of rock is not good, then you are mistaken. A rock with such a growth will help marine life. This rock can be obtained from a sea and a coral reef.

The live rock is known to have ample bacteria on it. These bacteria can cut through various dangerous pollutants, thus making the water better for the cephalopods.

For example, the nitrate cycle can be easily broken by the bacteria that grow on the live rock. This will help you to cycle the tank well. The pollutants can be easily rid of.

3. Filtration

Filtration is one of the most important parts of the Octopus tank. It is often referred to as a life support system. If your filtration fails in the water tank, there is no way you can save your Octopus.

If you have a fish of the same weight as your pet Octopus, you can expect your pet Octopus to produce almost three times of the waste that fish will produce. This only means that the filtration system for an Octopus needs to be stronger and sturdier.

When you are setting up a filtration system for your pet Octopus, you will find many options for the same. It is important to understand all these systems in great detail so that you can make the right choice.

This section will help you to make an informed choice when you are setting up a filtration system for the Octopus tank. This will help you to do the best thing possible for your Octopus.

A filter relies on its nitrogen cycle. This is what you should be looking at installing in your water tank.

It should be noted that under gravel filtration can't work well for an Octopus aquarium. An Octopus will dig and disturb the filtration system. It will also try to spoil the tubes. This will disrupt the entire filtration system.

It should be understood that carbon is considered very important for all water tanks. The carbon can absorb various ejects such as ink. There are some species of Octopuses that can eject the same.

Carbon is also capable of absorbing all the extra waste that the water could be carrying. Sometimes, extra waste can make the water look yellowish. This can be undone by carbon.

Aquarium substrate

When you have an aquarium, you will have to make a decision as to what to do with the aquarium substrate. There are many debates on this particular topic.

The best thing that you can do with the aquarium substrate is to keep a thin layer as aquarium sand. It is very easy to clean this thin layer. It is also important to note that the sand does not get clogged with waste material.

When you buy sand for your water tank, you will have many options. There is a special coral sand that is available is most shops. It is better to avoid this sand as the cephalopod is very sensitive to this kind of sand.

The coral sand is known to be very coarse. It is better to use fine sand. This kind of sand is not abrasive to the Octopus' skin. It is better to use a depth of over one inch.

It should be noted that certain species of Octopus need a greater depth of sand. This is important so that they can hide and rest well. You can increase the depth according to the species that you are looking to buy.

Understanding the water parameters

You should know that most Octopuses live in pure seawater 33 – 36 ppt. Also, the temperature for the species ranges from 6°C to 11°C. There is evidence that temperatures between 12 and 13°C are harmful over long periods.

Roland Anderson is pushing for aquariums to keep them cooler, as low as is practical for the chilling unit. Evidence from the Alaska Sealife Center in Sward, Alaska shows that Octopuses can live up to five years at 5-8°C, giving aquariums longer to exhibit, train and show individual animals, and cutting down the expense of acquiring a new animal every year.

Of course this will lead to more expenses of running the chiller unit and will lead to more condensation on the glass of a tank, but it should be offset by lower expense of animal acquisition. They are not at all tolerant to sudden changes in temperature and well maintained highly reliable chilling equipment is essential for keeping this species.

It is also important that chillers and heat exchangers are made from non-corrosive materials, as metals (especially copper) are extremely dangerous to Octopus. Titanium is a suitable alternative. Temperatures of 12°C lead to increased activity and can lead to animals jetting and damaging the mantle – this doesn't always but can result in infection and possible death so is to be avoided.

Ammonia levels should be zero and Nitrate levels should be ≤ 0.3 mg/l. GPO's are able to withstand elevated concentrations of Nitrate as high as 50ppt but again should not stay at these levels for a long time. A base level should range from 0 to 25 mg/l.

Phosphate also does not seem to be critical to Octopuses. Octopuses prefer slightly alkaline pH levels; 7.5 – 8. Rapid pH changes can stress Octopuses. Dissolved Oxygen Water should be well aerated but not supersaturated; 85-104.

Natural sea water seems to provide best results when keeping an Octopus. According to Kerry Perkins of Brighton Sealife Centre, certain brands of artificial sea water have caused problems with Cephalopods in the past, lack of certain micronutrients in the artificial make up can cause deformed growth in statolith's, although more studies need to be done.

Octopuses are sensitive to metal concentrations; particularly copper and tin (as are all molluscs).

4. Hiding place

Public aquariums use various kinds of enrichment devices. These have been used for years. It should be noted that an Octopus can easily open lids and covers. They are intelligent and smart enough to do so.

There are many public aquariums around the world that house Octopuses. These aquariums have had incidents where the Octopus has opened various lids. There is a special kind of box that is used to keep the food of the Octopus. This box is called the octobox.

It should be noted here that an Octopus is capable of opening these boxes to get its food. The Octopus easily opens the box and takes out the food. There are many public aquariums that have these boxs with simple lathes. The Octopus easily learns to open the latches of the octobox.

It can be very scary for a live animal, such as a crab to watch an animal opening the latch. So, avoid using such animals in the box of the animal.

There are some special lollies that are manufactured for the Octopus. You can use these lollies in the octobox. The Octopus will enjoy the treat and live animals can be speared.

Octopuses love hiding places. In their natural habitat, they have many hiding places. It is important that you provide the same when they are in captivity in your home.

An Octopus loves a hiding place. They will use this place to hide, rejuvenate and rest. You can create small hiding places in the water tank of the Octopus.

It is important that you use only safe materials to create the hiding places. You can make use of rocks and pipes to create such spaces. It is also important that you don't leave anything hanging.

Safety of the Octopus is your duty. It is important to make sure that the Octopus is not hurt by the hiding place or any other thing in the aquarium. Make sure that there is nothing that can prick the Octopus.

Many people prefer using a large number of live rocks in the water tank. This allows them to create many small hiding places. The benefit of these hiding areas is that the bacteria on the live rocks are beneficial for the Octopus.

It is important to understand the importance of hiding spaces for the Octopuses. There are some people who keep only one or two rocks in the aquarium. They believe that the Octopus should be visible to them all the time.

Another suggestion that you can use while constructing the water tank is to make caves of different sizes for the Octopus. This will help the Octopus as it grows in size and dimensions.

You should make caves in a way that the Octopus finds it easy to crawl inside them. There should be small holes that will help the Octopus to peer outside from those holes in the caves.

It is important that the Octopus is safe and sound. He needs to feel secure. Even if he is visible to you all the time, he might feel distressed and insecure. This is not right for the overall growth of the pet. Hiding places will help him feel secure. So, it is important that you provide many hiding places for your Octopus in the water tank.

5. Heater

While you are setting up your water tank for the Octopus, you might also have to place a heater inside the water tank. This will help to regulate the temperature of the water in the tank.

It should be noted that the place you reside in will affect the need of a heater. It is important that you understand the weather conditions in your area before you make a choice regarding the heater.

The choice of Octopus will also affect the choice of a heater. You should understand that different species of Octopuses have different requirements, even in terms of water temperature.

In most cases, a heater and thermostat are used in combination in the water tank. This particular combination is required to keep the water at the right and also constant temperature.

You will also need a thermometer to monitor the temperature of the water. It is important that the thermometer is accurate. You should also take into account the size of the water tank when you are finalizing a water heater.

You should get a thermometer installed inside the aquarium of the animal. It is important that you check the thermometer regularly and make sure that the temperature is being maintained.

There are some people who install heaters for their entire home. But, this is not a very good idea because it will cost more and you will have to bear temperature ranges that you might not want to.

You can look at installing ceramic heat emitters or space emitters. It is important that the heater is installed perfectly so that there are no fire related incidents.

If you are planning on using heat pads to keep the pet warm then you should know that a heat pad can keep the thing that it is in contact with warm, but it can't heat the air and water.

When we are talking about maintaining a consistent temperature for the pet Octopus, we are essentially talking about maintaining the temperature of the water. The water needs to warm and be maintained at a certain temperature.

You can use a heat pad for extra warmth if needed. If your pet is not well or if you are trying to take him out of hibernation, you can keep the heat pad under the bed of the pet.

The heat pad will provide extra warmth to the pet and will help him to heal faster. But, don't rely on a heat pad to keep the temperature of the cage consistent.

You should be careful when you have heaters installed in your home or in the aquarium of the pet Octopus. Your smoke alarms should be in good condition. You should also make sure that the Octopus can't get to the heat source. These all are precautions that you should take.

Space heater

There are many kinds of space heaters available on the market. You have the option of oil based space heaters to infrared heaters. These heaters are portable and easy to handle.

Space heaters are very easy to install. They come with a thermostat. The heater needs to be plugged in to the socket and the desired temperature needs to be set.

In comparison to a CHE, they are more expensive. The old models were not very safe, but the newer ones come with an auto shut option, which makes them quite safe.

Ceramic heat emitter or CHE

A ceramic heat emitter is another popular choice of owners to give their Octopuses a consistent temperature range. The CHE looks like a light bulb.

You can easily fix it like a light bulb. It is like a bulb that emits no light but generates heat. You will also have to purchase a CHE lamp to plug into the emitter and a thermostat to regulate the temperature.

You can easily buy a CHE online. It is an excellent choice for heating the tank of the pet animal, though it might not be suitable if you want to heat a room.

6. Lighting

Subdued lighting using LED or fluorescent tubes is sufficient – Use of red light gives an un-natural appearance and has no known benefit as Octopuses are able to adapt to low levels of white lighting. It has been observed in several aquariums that when regularly given enrichment during the daytime they will switch to being very active during daylight hours.

An incident at the Sea Star aquarium, Cobourg, Germany where a GPO managed to extinguish a 2000w metal halide lamp by squirting a jet of water at it out of the top of the tank suggests that this level of lighting is too bright.

Artificial light

While you can't control when the sun rises and sets, you can provide adequate artificial light in the aquarium of the pet. This will ensure that the pet gets consistent lights.

Some owners think that it is enough to make sure that the Octopus is exposed to constant temperature. They believe that light cycle is not a crucial thing for an Octopus.

You should know that this is absolutely false. If you don't expose your animal to consistent light cycles, he will try to attempt hibernation, and in the process put himself into danger.

You can make use of desk lamp, reptile lamp or normal room light. You don't need a special kind of light. It just needs to be some light source.

You can manually switch the light on and off at approximately the same time to make sure that a consistent cycle is maintained. The problem with this system is that there is a chance of you forgetting to switch the light on.

A simpler way to take care of the light cycles is to set a timer. You can set it for a time period of twelve to fourteen hours. This system is more efficient and less troublesome for you.

7. Aeration

Oxygen levels in an Octopus display need to be high. Fortunately, cool water naturally holds more oxygen which is one reason why Giant Pacific Octopuses are so much larger than their tropical cousins.

Using air diffusers in GPO tanks are not a good way to achieve this as the air bubbles can get caught in the web and mantle – stretching the skin and sometimes ripping the webbing. Movement of water through the filtration system should agitate or replace (through overflow) the surface constantly to ensure oxygenation.

Gas saturation is dangerous to Giant Pacific Octopuses – any breaks in the pipework on the suction side of the pump can potentially cause supersaturation.

It is always recommended that screens should be installed on the tank. This will prevent the Octopus from escaping the tank. This is simple way to avoid such incidents.

These screens can also avoid the incidents of overflowing. When the overflow occurs, there can be a blockage. This can be very detrimental for the Octopus. It is important to prevent such incidents.

You should use chicken mesh for the water tank. It is important that plastic is used. This will also be useful for the Octopus because the overflow can be stopped.

8. Flash Photography

Repeated flash from visitors seems to have a negative effect on an Octopus, making it less likely to be active during the day, and sometimes causing visible flinching. No actual health problems have been linked to flash photography, however most aquariums now ban flash photography and this is particularly important with this species.

Limited amounts don't seem to put off a friendly Octopus during play time, though. Negative effects are far more likely to be seen when an animal is nearing senescence or guarding eggs.

9. Environmental and behavioural enrichment

Live food is important not only for dietary reasons but also as a form of enrichment. Brittle stars and other echinoderms may also provide enrichment. Making sure that the display is as naturalistic as possible with plenty of rocks and fake seaweeds for the Octopus to move around helps to keep them occupied.

A flow of water into the tank also seems to be appreciated by some individuals. Regular interaction with keepers seems to be actively enjoyed by all Giant Pacific Octopuses, except for those who have reached senescence.

Incorporating regular Octopus enrichment feeds into the daily talks schedule ensures that the Octopus is being regularly interacted with. At these events the Octopus has the opportunity to display a behaviour that is only usually associated with vertebrate animals.

Some individual Giant Pacific Octopuses really seem to enjoy rough play and will cling onto a keepers arm allowing it to be pulled right out of the water. At BRA Newquay a GPO named Mr Tickle loved being tickled with a frayed polypropylene rope so much so that he would let go completely of the edges of the tank and could be spun around and around in the centre of the tank.

It is not uncommon for a friendly Octopus to enjoy wrestling so much that it refuses to eat, even if it is hungry until it is sure the aquarist has packed up and closed the lid. As well as hands on interaction, toys and other enrichment devices can also be used to keep the Octopuses' environment changing and to keep them working for their food. Public aquariums use various kinds of enrichment devices. These have been used for years.

There are many public aquariums around the world that house Octopuses. These aquariums have had incidents where the Octopus has opened various lids. There is a special kind of box that is used to keep the food of the Octopus. This box is called the octobox.

It should be noted here that an Octopus is capable of opening these boxes to get its food. The Octopus easily opens the box and takes out the food. There are many public aquariums that have these boxs with simple lathes. The Octopus easily learns to open the latches of the octobox.

Chapter 6: Diet requirements of the Octopus

As the owner or as the prospective owner of an Octopus, it should be your foremost concern to provide adequate and proper nutrition to the pet. If the pet animal in deficient in any nutrient, he will develop various deficiencies and acquire many diseases.

When the nutrition is right, you can easily ward off many dangerous diseases. Each animal species is different. Just because certain kinds of foods are good for your pet dog, it does not mean that they will be good for other pets also.

It is important to learn about all the foods that the pet animal is naturally inclined towards. You should always be looking at maintaining good health of your pet.

It is important to learn about the foods that are good for your pet. But, you should also understand that the foods that you feed your pet which could be lacking in certain nutrients. An animal in the wild is different from one in captivity. Availability of certain foods will also affect the diet of your pet.

Generally, the food given to captive pets is lacking in certain nutrients. It is not able to provide the pet with all the necessary nutrients. In such a case, you will have to give commercial pellets to your pet. These pellets are known to compensate for the various nutritional deficiencies that the animal might have due to malnutrition.

You should always aim at providing wholesome nutrition to your pet. It is important to understand the pet's nutritional requirements and include all the nutrients in his daily meals. To meet his nutritional requirements, you might also have to give him certain supplements.

The supplements will help you to make up for the essential nutrients that are not found in his daily meals. Though these supplements are easily available, you should definitely consult a veterinarian before you give your pet any kind of supplements.

It is very important that you serve only high quality food to your pet. If you are trying to save some money by buying cheaper, low quality alternatives, then you are in a bad situation. A low quality food will affect the health of the pet.

You can expect him to acquire deficiencies and diseases if he is not fed good quality food. The cure for this is taking the pet to the veterinarian. This in turn will only cost you more money. To avoid this endless loop, it is better to work on the basics. Keep the pet healthy by feeding him with high quality foods, rather than spending money on him by taking him to the veterinarian.

The diet of the Octopus will have a direct effect on the way he feels and functions. You should make sure that the staple diet of the pet is able to provide him with all the necessary nutrients.

The Octopus will also enjoy the treats that you serve him. Maintain a good balance between the staple items and treats. You can choose from various food items, such as crabs, shrimps, small fishes, scallops, snails and mussels to provide wholesome nutrition to the pet.

If you are unable to provide the pet Octopus the food that he normally survives on, then he will not be able to survive well. So, it is better not to replicate the diet of other pets.

1. The nutritional requirement of the Octopus

People still don't know much about the nutritional requirements of the Octopus. There are lot of studies and research that are still being done to understand the nutritional requirements of the Octopus. Some believe that keeping the diet simple and close to the diet of a wild Octopus if good for the animal.

It is important that you don't experiment with the diet of the pet animal. You can't feed him anything that you wish to. This is not good for the health of the pet.

If you are expecting that your pet Octopus can live on a diet that a pet dog lives on, you are only making things difficult for the pet Octopus. You will regret it later, so better to be careful for the Octopus.

You should try to provide certain staples in the everyday food of the Octopus. These staples are crabs, shrimps, small fish, scallops, snails and mussels. You should also make sure that the food that you choose to serve is of a good quality.

The owners have the choice of feeding various commercial foods to the pet cephalopod. It is important to check all the ingredients of commercial foods to be sure that the food is safe for the pet Octopus.

You should never go by the brand picture to buy your pet's food. It is important to check the main ingredients and percentage of each ingredient.

It is better if the main ingredient of these foods is meat. You should avoid any food that has by-products of animals instead of the real food. You should also avoid food with ingredients such as BHT, BHA and ethoxyquin.

A pet Octopus is usually served pieces of seafood as its main food. Wholesome seafood is a nutritious meal that is ground into bite sized pellets for the pets.

When you are buying seafood, you should also look for the ideal shape and size. The pet Octopus might not be able to eat a bigger size, and might even choke on it.

You can look for simpler shapes and sizes rather than fancy ones. If the size of the pieces is small, they are easier to eat and swallow, which is ideal for the pet Octopus.

You should also make sure that the percentage content of each nutrient is just right for the Octopus. It has been discovered that less protein in the diet of the pet can lead to various diseases and disorders.

The percentage of fat in the diet of the pet Octopus will depend on the individual needs of your pet. If your pet Octopus looks sluggish, you might want to lower the fat in his diet.

If you are looking to feed your pet Octopus simple yet good food then you can go for commercial seafood along with some occasional mussels as a treat. These treats will provide the necessary fibre in the diet of the pet.

Shrimps are also considered to be highly nutritious for the pet Octopus. It is believed that it is better than many other foods, but if the food pieces are bigger, it can be difficult for the pet Octopus.

An ideal pet Octopus diet would consist of up 25-30 per cent of protein, 10-15 per cent of fat, 40 per cent of carbohydrates, 10-15 per cent of fibre and minimum of 2 per cent of vitamins and minerals.

The protein in the diet can be primarily given by fish, shrimp and other meat. The main source of food for an Octopus can be shrimp. It is enough to provide it all the necessary nutrients.

The fat in the diet can be primarily given by various shrimps and fish. They are good sources of fat. Various oils also help to keep the fat content optimal in the diet of the Octopus.

The carbohydrate in the diet is supplemented by grains, vegetables and fruits. On the other hand, the fibre in the diet is supplemented by grains, insects, vegetables and fruits.

To meet his nutritional requirements, you might also have to give him certain supplements. The supplements will help you to make up for the essential nutrients that are not found in his daily meals.

Though these supplements are easily available, you should definitely consult a veterinarian before you give your Octopus any kind of supplements.

You also have the option of giving commercial marine food to your pet animal. But, it should be noted that no such food is complete in its nutritional requirement.

It is often believed that most commercial Octopus foods are only equivalent to low quality sea food in their nutritional content. This is not good for the pet animal's overall development. They contain big pieces of seafood, which are difficult for the pet animal to take in.

2. Food requirements of the Octopus

As discussed in the previous section, you can look at including good quality sea food or commercial food as the main food of the pet Octopus.

There has always been a debate about the right food for the pet Octopus. The pet Octopus's diet is not so different from the wild one that it is all the more important to understand it well.

It is always recommended that the everyday diet of the pet Octopus is closely worked out with a vet. This will help you to provide optimal nutrition to the pet animal.

You can also save yourself from making some big blunders. It is not a good idea to mess up a pet's diet in the name of experimenting.

You have to be sure before you can serve a food item to the pet. It is better that you spend some time in understanding the food requirements of the pet Octopus. This will allow you to do the best for him.

The requirements of the Octopus will change as he grows in age. The requirements will vary based on the age and also health of the animal.

If you find it cumbersome to cut sea food into small sizes, you can cut a big batch and freeze it. You can also look for places that offer small sized sea food for the pet.

You should aim at providing all the necessary nutrients to the pet through his food. In such a case, you can avoid giving any extra supplements to the pet animal.

At times, your pet's diet might not be able to provide it with the right set of nutrients and vitamins. In such a case, avoid administering any medicines on your own.

It is always better to consult a veterinarian before you administer any supplements to the Octopus. You should also discuss the dosage with the veterinarian.

If the pet is not well and is recuperating from an injury or disease, the veterinarian might advise you to administer certain supplements to the pet. These supplements will help the pet to heal faster and get back on his feet sooner.

You should also make sure that the treat foods also provide some nutrition to the animal. While you can be sure that your pet is getting the right nutrients, the pet can enjoy the treat given to him.

You can also include supplements of fatty acids in the diet of the pet. A few drops of this kind of supplement will enhance the taste and the nutritional value of the food item that is being served to the pet animal.

While it can be necessary to supplement certain vitamins and nutrients to the pet, you should also be aware of the hazards of over feeding a certain nutrient. If there is an overdose of a certain vitamin in the body of the animal, it can lead to vitamin toxicity.

You might even see that your pet is enjoying all the treats, but this in no way means that you can give him an overdose. You should always do what is right for the health of the Octopus.

Octopuses feed themselves on clams, fish and shrimps in their natural habitat. Many owners wonder whether it is necessary to feed the pet Octopus clams.

You can choose to serve clams to a pet animal, but it is not necessary. If the pet is being served high quality nutritional food, he can do without the clams.

The main benefit of adding clams in the pet's diet is that they will add a lot of fibre and protein in the pet's diet. Eating shrimps and clams also gives the pet the mental stimulation of being in his natural habitat.

If you decide to feed shrimps and clams to the Octopus, then you should look for small sized shrimps and clams. They should also be cleaned properly. These animals are safe and healthy for the pet animal.

Make sure that the seafood that you serve is not dirty or unhealthy. Such food items aren't very hygienic because of their poor sanitary conditions. Such a feed will only make the pet sick.

It is important to know where the food comes from. If you are oblivious about such things, you can never control what goes in the water tank.

Your lax attitude can make your pet sick. You have to make sure that the sea food is disease free before you feed it to the pet Octopus.

The only way to ensure that healthy food is being served to the pet is to know where the food is coming from. It is better to spend some extra money and get good quality food than to compromise on the health of the pet.

3. How does an Octopus eat?

People who have never domesticated Octopuses wonder as to how they eat their food. Octopuses look very different, and this question can be bothersome for many people.

If you are interested in knowing how an Octopus eats his food, this section will be helpful for you. The Octopus uses a body structure called beak to eat its food. Beak is a hardened body structure found in most cephalopods.

A beak can be compared to a finger nail. It is located in a body muscle.

When an Octopus is catching its prey for food it billows the entire body. The beak is then used to attack and bite the prey at hand.

The beak is so hard and tough that it can be used to easily crush down exoskeletons and bones. This can help you understand the power of a cephalopod's beak.

4. How much to feed the Octopus?

As a pet parent, you will have a hard time wondering as to how much food you should feed your pet animal. You don't want to over feed. And, at the same time you don't want to leave him hungry. This can be tricky for any pet parent.

It is important that enough emphasis is laid on this particular point. If you are thinking that you need to feed the Octopus three to four times a day, then you are wrong. The Octopus does not need so much food.

The ideal scenario for the Octopus is if you serve him good quality shrimp once a day for six days a week. Many people don't give food to the Octopus for one day in the week. This helps the Octopus to stay healthy and digest his food well.

5. Can an Octopus eat itself?

If you are new to the world of cephalopods, then you should know that Octopuses can eat their arms. This phenomenon is known as autophagy or self-cannibalism.

An important thing that needs to be understood here is that Octopuses don't do so out of hunger. An Octopus will eat its arm if it is stressed.

Stress in cephalopods is very harmful for their health and well-being. A stressed Octopus will contribute towards his declining health. He would do things that will only add to his misery.

Good and healthy food is a contributor to total well-being. So, it is important that you give importance to wholesome food. This can be simply to minimize stress in Octopuses.

6. Locating a source of crabs and shrimps for the Octopus

It should be noted that a young Octopus will need more food as compared to an older one. You should make sure that you don't give less food to your younger Octopus. Also, don't feed too much food to your older Octopus.

A small Octopus will eat smaller foods such as shrimps, fiddler crabs, hermit crabs, amphipods from live rocks and small pieces of good quality seafood.

Most young Octopuses can eat snails. You might be surprised to know that Octopuses will enjoying clams and mussels.

7. Treats

You should also offer treats to the pet animal every now and then. It is important that the treats are healthy. They should not disturb the nutritional balance of the pet.

If you keep serving him the wrong kinds of treats, it will only affect his health in the long run. It is also important that the pet associates the treat with reward. He should know that he is being served the treat reward for a reason.

You will have to keep a check on the amount of treats a pet will get. This is important because treats are not food replacements. They are only small rewards.

You should always look for treats that are healthy for the pet. The pet should enjoy eating them, but their nutrition should not be compromised.

When you serve the treat, you need to make sure that you don't add any extra salt or sugar. Also, make sure that you cut the food item into small pieces. It will be easier for the Octopus to eat it.

It should be noted that just because your pet animal seems to enjoy a treat, you can't give the food item to him all day long. You will have to keep a check on the amount of treats an octopus will get. This is important because treats are not food replacements.

If you keep serving him the wrong kinds of treats, it will only affect his health in the long run. The pet can suffer from diarrhoea and other disorders and problems because of consuming wrong food items. This is the last thing that you would want as a parent of the pet.

This section will help you understand various kinds of treats that you can serve your pet. The best kind of treat for a pet Octopus is a food item that has meat as its main component. Octopuses will love it, and it is also healthy for them.

Fresh scallops can serve as a very good treat for the pet Octopus. It is good for the pet and is also delicious for him. It is important that only healthy items are served as treat items.

8. Foods that should be avoided

There are certain food items that should be avoided for the Octopus. This section will help you understand these food items.

Keep the food simple and healthy. If you are giving fish, then you should make sure that it does not have bones because the bones can get stuck.

Your pet wouldn't know that these foods are not good for him. You should take it upon yourself to keep such foods away from the pet.

If you are looking for a comprehensive list of food items that are unhealthy for the pet Octopus, then the given list will help you. You should try to avoid these food items:

- **Gold fish**: If you are serving fish as the main source food for the pet Octopus, you should remember that it is best to avoid gold fish. It is important that you avoid this food type in any form whatsoever.

- **Feeder fish**: If you are serving fish as the main source food for the pet Octopus, you should remember that it is best to avoid feeder fish. It is important that you avoid this food type in any form whatsoever.

- **Artemia or brine shrimp**: This kind of food item is not an ideal source of protein. It is advised to avoid it while you are deciding on for items for the pet Octopus. Many young Octopuses have shown severe consequences after consuming this kind of food item.

- **Sweeteners**: It is important to avoid corn syrup and sugar coated food.

- **Artificial preservatives**: They will add nothing to the diet of the pet. And, they are not good in the long run.

- **By-products**: You should always try to give the pet the real thing. There is no need to serve by-products.

- **Caffeine**: Sometimes, the children of the house can force the pet to consume such food items just for some fun. So, it is important that you keep a check on what the kids are doing when they are with the Octopus.

- **Citrus fruits**: Citrus fruits such as lemons, pineapple, oranges and limes are not suitable for a pet Octopus.

- **Chocolates**: Chocolates are unhealthy for these animals. You should make sure that you keep these food items away from your Octopus.

- **Raisins and grapes**: Grapes and raisins are toxic for the pet. If these food items are given for a longer duration, substantial damage is done to his health.

- **Peanuts:** Another food item that is dangerous for the pet is the peanuts. Other legumes should also not be given to the pet animal. They can cause choking and vomiting pet.

- **Foods high in salt**: You should try not to feed foods that are very rich in salt content. You should keep all human junk food such as salted chips and nuts away from the pet Octopus.

Chapter 7: Taking care of your Octopus's health

It is important that you take care of your pet's health. The pet will depend on you for most of its needs. It will not be able to tell you if it is facing any discomfort regarding its health. You should be able to identify the symptoms of various diseases in your pet to treat it well.

If you take care of the diet of the pet, you can save him from many deadly diseases. You should make sure that the pet lives in a healthy environment. These simple things will help you to keep the pet healthy.

You should also be able to diagnose any symptoms of injuries in your pet. If you can treat him in your home, then you should do it very carefully. In case you have any doubts, you should take the pet to the vet.

Maintaining the health of the Octopus would always be your primary concern as the owner. The food that you give him, his environment, his hygiene levels, everything will ultimately affect his health conditions.

This chapter will help you to understand simple ways to keep the Octopus healthy. You will also learn about the common health problems that can affect your Octopus.

You should always make sure that your pet Octopus is always kept in a clean environment. A neat and clean environment will help you to keep away many common ailments and diseases.

You should understand the various health related issues that your pet can suffer from. This knowledge will help you to get the right treatment at the right time.

It is also important that you understand how you can take care of a sick pet. This knowledge will help you to keep you calm and help the sick animal in the best way possible. Proper care will help him to get better faster.

1. When should you see the veterinarian?

If you find your pet behaving differently from normal, then the first step you should take is to provide him with warmth. It is important that the pet is not cold and the proper temperature is maintained.

Even after that if you see him deteriorating, it is time to see the veterinarian. If the condition is not very severe, you can book an appointment in the next three to four days.

But if there is an emergency, you should not waste time and should take the Octopus to the veterinarian as soon as possible. You can also take him to the emergency clinic in your locality.

It is important that you are able to identify the signs of emergency in your pet so that you can act without delay. If you happen to notice the following in your pet Octopus, you should know that it is an emergency and the veterinarian needs to be consulted:

- **Lethargy**: If the pet is not moving at all, try to increase the heat for him. If the pet remains to be unresponsive even after that, this can be serious. Don't do something drastic such as putting a stick in the water bed. Just take him to the doctor.

- **Diarrhoea**: If the problem of diarrhoea or green stools persists for more than two days, you will have to get the faecal exam done for any complications. After you have domesticated an Octopus for a while, you will be able to identify normal faeces and loose faeces.

- **Blood**: Blood from an arm or a small cut is not a thing to worry about. But, blood from urine is a cause of serious concern. It can get critical if not treated on time.

- **Vomits**: You might be surprised to learn that Octopuses can vomit like many other animals. Any undigested food is immediately vomited. Vomits caused by poisoning, choking or sickness should not be ignored at any cost. You should be able to identify the vomit of the Octopus so that you can take an action.

- If you see the pet gasping for breath, or if you notice twitching or abnormal movements of limbs, you should consult the veterinarian as soon as possible.

Though it is always advised to take the pet to the vet if any health problem arises, it is always a great idea to keep a first aid kit ready. This will help in the case of minor injuries and also emergencies when you can't reach the vet.

The main aim of first aid is to give the pet some relief from his pain. Giving first aid will not be very difficult if you follow the right steps in the right order.

While you are giving the animal some first aid, there are a few things that you should do. This will help you to calm the Octopus and also give him the necessary aid.

You should make sure that you don't aggravate the pain and misery of the poor animal in any way. You should follow the given procedures in the given order to help the Octopus.

You should make sure that the airway of the animal is not blocked. Make sure that the Octopus is able to breathe properly.

After you have made sure that the animal is breathing properly, it is important to check if he is bleeding. If the animal is bleeding, you should take the necessary steps to stop his bleeding.

You should also be able to examine how profusely he is bleeding. After you have succeeded in reducing the bleeding of the Octopus, you have to take the necessary steps to maintain the right temperature of the pet animal.

If the body temperature is not maintained, it will worsen the condition of the pet. You should understand that pet a Octopus is easily prone to stress. Injury and pain are two factors that can stress him a lot.

So, it is important that you take the necessary steps to reduce his stress levels. This might seem like an impossible and daunting task, but if you take the right steps, you will be able to calm your animal successfully.

When you keep a first aid kit, it is important that you have knowledge about each item. You should know how to use things. You should also replace stuff when they reach their expiration date.

The various items that the first aid box of the Octopus should have are bottled water, hand warmers, paper towels, flash light, toilet paper, scissors, tweezers, cotton swabs, hydrogen peroxide, saline water, Neosporin and ensure.

When you are giving first aid to your pet, you should check their body temperature. They should neither be too hot or too cold. The cephalopods need to maintain a warm body temperature at all times. When they are stressed or injured, it is all the more important for them to maintain a warm body temperature.

Cephalopods have a lower body temperature when compared to the body temperature of the human beings. You should check the temperature of the animal. If he is hypothermic, you should make arrangements to keep him warm from the outside.

You should make sure that the pet is not overheated. Too much heat is not good for your pet. It can disrupt many normal functions of the Octopus. If the pet is overheated, make sure that you cool him down.

This step becomes all the more important when you are dealing with cephalopods. They will be unable to regulate their temperature. So, when you provide them with first aid, you will have to regulate their body temperature.

2. Maintaining records

It is advised to maintain regular health records for your pet. This will help you to understand his health in a better way. You would be able to detect even the smallest of issues with the help of these records.

For example, if you have a record of his size, you can notice any changes in the pet's weight. A drastic change in weight is often understood as an early symptom for diseases.

The pet can be saved from future health issues by keeping a simple record. If you can't keep a daily record, aim for a weekly record. Record all the important parameters at the beginning of each week and compare with the previous week.

The parameters that you should be aiming to record are the weight of the pet, the physical activity of the pet and the food intake of the pet.

You can calculate the quantity of food that the pet consumes by counting the number of kibble or by weighing the food that you serve and then the food that is left.

You can record the physical activity by observing and estimating the time. You should also look out for any gunk formation or lump formation on the body of the pet.

A lethargic pet that shows no interest in movement is not a good sign. You will only know these things if you observe. If you notice any change in the pet's normal activity levels or weight, you should be alerted.

This definitely means that something is wrong with the pet. An early action can save you from many health problems in the pet. This is good both for you and the pet.

3. Diagnosing injuries in the Octopus

Octopuses, like the other invertebrates, lead a very active lifestyle. They like moving around. Your pet is likely to spend most of its time doing so. This makes it susceptible to injuries.

There is nothing to worry about if your pet injures itself. You should be able to diagnose the injuries so that they can be treated well. You might even have to call the doctor from the doctor's clinic.

It is important that you learn the basics of diagnosing the injuries. This is important because if a small injury is treated well, the animal can be saved from a major problem in the future.

It is important that you understand that your pet animal might not show any signs of injuries, even when it is injured. It will be your responsibility to diagnose the injury before it turns into a bigger problem.

Looking for the symptoms of injuries

You should be on the lookout for any symptoms that your Octopus might display when it is injured. These symptoms could mean that there is something wrong with your Octopus. You should look carefully for the following symptoms:

-   Is your Octopus looking very disturbed? This could be because he is in pain.

-   Is your pet looking very lazy and lethargic? This could be because he has injured himself and is in pain.

-   Is the pet showing uncoordinated movements?

-   The pet could be having frequent or infrequent fits.

-   If there is a change in the way he carries himself, then this could also mean that the injury has forced the pet to change the way he usually is.

-   You should look out for the faeces of the animal. If there is any change in the colour of the faeces, this could mean that there is something wrong with his health.

- Do you spot any blood on the skin of the animal? You should look for blood in the enclosure of the animal also. This could mean that something is not right.

- Look for certain common symptoms, such as coughing and vomiting by the animal.

- Do you witness any changes in the skin of the pet? If yes, then this could also mean that there is something that needs your attention.

- If your pet looks scared and tense, you should understand that it is for a reason. You need to closely examine him to find out what is wrong.

When you spot any of the given symptoms in your pet, you should know that something is not right. You will have to take a closer look at the pet and examine. This examination will help you to understand if there is something wrong with your pet.

While you are examining your pet, you should also understand that your pet could be scared. It is important that you make the pet feel comfortable. This will help you conduct the examination properly and without any problems.

To make sure that the pet animal is not terrified when you are trying to examine him for any potential injuries, you can do the following:

You should make sure that you conduct the examination in a closed area, a place where the animal feels safe and protected. You should try to examine him indoors.

Do not let the place be crowded when the examination is being conducted. Make sure that all the other pets and your family members are outside and not in the same place where the examination is being conducted.

The noise level around you should be as low as possible. The noise will stress the pet and will irritate him, so make sure there is no noise around. Conduct the examination in a quiet place.

Be as gentle and kind as possible. This will help your pet to relax and feel less stressed. You should in no way add to the stress and pain of the pet.

If the animal will see you being fidgety, it will only add to his stress. You should be as calm and as confident as possible. Your confidence will give him some hope and relief.

Make sure that all the tools that are needed for the examination are ready. You shouldn't leave your pet alone to fetch the tools. Everything should be ready before the examination.

You should check his entire body. Remember to check on both sides of the body. Start the examination at one particular point and then move ahead from that point. The examination should be definite and guided and not random.

Look at how your pet responds to the body examination being done. If you feel that the animal is not taking it too well, you should stop the examination. You should look for any stress signs that he displays. You should not ignore them; otherwise the animal can go into deep shock.

4. Stress in Octopuses

If the Octopus does not get proper heat and light, he can go into stress mode. His senses start to shut down. It should be noted that hibernation is not good for pet Octopuses.

When the surroundings get very cold for the pet and the daylight shortens, the Octopus's body starts reacting differently. This is not natural for them.

After years and years of captivity, the Octopuses have also changed. They are dependent on consistent warm temperatures for their well-being. Their bodies are not suitable to bear extremely cold weather or extremely hot weather.

When there is a decrease in temperature or change in light cycles, the Octopus will panic. But, the body will give up very soon.

If too much time is lost, the Octopus will not be able to come out of the state. You can even lose your Octopus. As the owner of the Octopus, it is important that you make sure that your pet does not go into this state. If this happen, things can get very complicated.

Your primary focus should be that the Octopus remains healthy. This can be done by maintaining warm temperatures around the Octopus.

You should make sure that there is a light cycle that is consistently maintained in the water tank of the pet. The water should also be at a consistent warm temperature.

You should also make an attempt to understand the signs of stress. If you see your pet going into that zone, you can make temperature and light changes in his surroundings to bring him back to normal.

If you could touch the stomach area of the pet, it will be cold. The pet might also act very unusual. These are warning signals that the pet is getting stressed and shouldn't be ignored at all.

The first thing that you should do after encountering such warning signals is to warm the Octopus. You should not increase the temperature all of a sudden. Do it gradually and consistently.

If you increase the temperature all of a sudden, the pet might go into a shock state. You can use a heater to warm the water tank, but the heater will need a lot of regulation so that it does not get too hot.

If the pet does not respond for a very long time, it is advised that you call the veterinarian. The immune system of the pet will also suffer when he is trying to recuperate. Once you have brought him back, you should take extra care of him.

Make sure he is away from anything that can make him sick. You should keep an eye on the pet and lookout for signals.

A simpler way to avoid the pet to get stressed again is to keep the temperature of the tank a few degrees more than what is normal for the Octopus.

Signs of stress

There are a few symptoms that will help you to identify stress in your pet. You should stop the body examination as soon as you spot any of these symptoms. The following signs will help you to identify stress:

- The pet will try to escape you when it is stressed. It will not let you come closer to him and will get irritated.

- The pet will show violent movements. For example, the pet will strongly thump his arms on the glass of the water tank.

- The animal will show a drastic change in its activity level. There are a few animals that will become extremely active, while others will become very lethargic. They will not move at all.

- The pet would be seen grinding its body parts tightly and also flicking them.

- He would make strange and loud noises from his mouth, when not grinding his teeth tightly.

- If you measure the body temperature of the animal, there will be a change in the body temperature of the animal.

- The animal could also hurt himself on purpose.

- The Octopus can eat its own arms when it is in stress. This is a self-cannibalism. It is very common in many species of Octopus.

- The animal would lick his various body parts, such as legs and feet.

- The young ones would show the symptom of diarrhoea. They will suffer from frequent and liquid stools.

- If the animal is not treated on time, you will see that his appetite decreases with time. It will decrease to a point that it will become difficult for the animal to carry on his daily tasks.

Reducing stress

At this juncture, you would want to reduce the amount of stress that your Octopus must be going through. It is important that you take all the necessary steps to make the Octopus feel safe and secure.

- If your pet is still very young, then you should keep his tank in a secure and closed area. This will fill him with warmth. This is like a reassurance to the animal that he can be safe and secure.

- You should make sure that your pet can rest well in a calm environment. Keep him away from any place of commotion.

- Make sure that there are no noises around the animal. Any kind of noise will disrupt him and will agitate him.

- You should also try your best to make sure that there are no sudden noises around the Octopus. The animal should be able to rest in a calm environment. Sudden noises and voices will disturb the pet and will agitate him further. It should be made certain that all the noises are eliminated.

5. Taking care of a senior Octopus

An Octopus of age four or five is said to be an elderly or senior Octopus. It is important to care for the pet as he grows old. He will show certain changes in his body and behaviour that you should be okay with.

It is not right to expect a senior Octopus to have the same energy levels as a younger one. The senior pet will exercise less, eat less and litter less. They will start becoming oblivious of their routine light schedule.

The pet will also show a decline in his capacity and eyesight. The pet will become lethargic. He will not have much energy and would prefer sleeping most of the time. He might want to spend most of his time hiding in the cave.

The Octopus will also be stressed easily. Please don't force an elderly cephalopod to act young. You have to let him be if you wish to see him happy. It is important that you don't keep unrealistic expectations from him.

There are a few things that you need to take care of. Make sure that the pet is not disturbed when he is hiding in one of the hiding places. You should be extra careful about the temperature of the water.

If you are using a heater, it is important to monitor it regularly. If the heater does not have an automatic shutdown, it can get too warm for the pet very quickly. This can be dangerous for the Octopus.

If the pet is losing excessive weight, feed him with fat rich food items. You should also make sure that he not disturbed by children of the house. This can irritate the Octopus.

Sometimes, children keep tapping on the glass of the aquarium. This can irritate the Octopus. You have to monitor the kids around the aquarium. Your main aim should be to provide good food to the pet and let him rest well.

If the pet is experiencing any kind of pain, you should consult the veterinarian. He might prescribe some pain relief medication. This will help the Octopus to get some relief and rest. Never administer any drugs without consultation.

Though the pet will not show much inclination towards moving around, you should encourage him to do some everyday.

It is important that you maintain daily health records of the pet. The pet should be healthy even when he is four years old. Schedule frequent visits to the veterinarian and make sure that the Octopus remains fit.

6. Common health problems of the Octopus

An unhealthy pet can be a nightmare for any owner. The last thing that you would want is to see your pet in pain. Many disease causing parasites dwell in unhygienic places and food.

If you take care of the hygiene and food of the Octopus, there are many diseases that you can be averted. You should always consult a vet when you find any unusual traits and symptoms in the pet.

You should make sure that the Octopus has all his food doses on time. Apart from this, you should take him for regular check-ups to the veterinarian. This is important so that even the smallest health issue can be tracked at an early stage.

At times, even after all the precautions that you take, the pet can get sick. It is always better to be well equipped so that you can help your pet.

A pet Octopus is prone to certain diseases such as rotten skin and various infections. If proper care is not taken, you will find your pet getting sick very often. Another point that needs to be noted here is that you will have to be extra vigilant to understand that something is wrong with the pet.

This section will help you to understand the various diseases that your pet can suffer from. The various symptoms and causes are also discussed in detail. This will help you to recognize a symptom, which could have otherwise gone unnoticed.

Though the section helps you to understand the various common health problems of the Octopus, it should be understood that a veterinarian should be consulted in case of any health related issue.

A veterinarian will physically examine the pet and suggest what is best for your pet animal.

When you are looking to maintain the health of your pet Octopus, then you should make an attempt to understand the common health issues that the animal faces. This will help you to prepare yourself well and also treat your pet well.

Understanding various diseases and their symptoms

Who wouldn't want their pets to be healthy? Nobody would want to see a helpless animal suffering from a disease. To make sure that your Octopus enjoys good health at all times, it is important that you recognize the symptoms of diseases that can affect an Octopus at an early stage.

If you can detect a disease in an early stage, there are more chances that the disease will be cured. To be able to do so, you should make an attempt to understand the various diseases that can affect an Octopus along with their symptoms.

It is known that Octopuses are not susceptible to diseases if they are given a good diet and given a good and clean environment. But, it is also known that Octopuses are easily stressed.

You should always make sure that your pet is always kept in a clean environment. A neat and clean environment will help you to keep off many common ailments and diseases.

There are some common health issues that your Octopus is prone to, such as tumours and cysts. There are many issues that might not start as a big problem, but become serious problems if not treated on time.

You should also never ignore any symptom that you see because an ignored symptom will lead to serious problems later. As in humans, an early detected problem or disease can be treated easily in Octopuses also.

The various diseases that your pet Octopus can suffer from are as follows:

Tumours and cysts

Your pet is at risk to various cysts and tumours. If you notice any bumps on the body of the Octopus, don't take it lightly. This can be dangerous.

It occurs because of the uncontrolled growth of the cells in the Octopus's body. Though this is very common in these animals, it can be difficult to detect, especially in the earlier stages.

It is known that older Octopuses are more at risk of such tumours and cysts. But, various tumours can also attack younger Octopuses.

You should never take any symptoms lightly and should visit the veterinarian when you observe changes in an Octopus. The veterinarian will conduct tests on the blood sample of the pet to confirm this health condition.

You can look out for the various common symptoms in the Octopus to know that he is suffering from this particular disease. You will notice a sudden and drastic weight loss in the pet.

You will notice the pet to be very lazy and lethargic. It will appear that he has no energy to do anything. The pet will have visible bumps and changes in the skin texture. The pet will suffer from diarrhoea. The lymph nodes of the pet will also be swollen.

Another symptom that could accompany this disease is tiredness. The pet will experience some difficulty in his breathing and will acquire extreme tiredness.

Treatment:

It is important that you take the pet to the veterinarian. He will be able to administer certain medicines and injections. The veterinarian might also suggest surgery.

It is very difficult to save the pet after he has been diagnosed with this a deadly tumour. Mostly, it gets detected in later stages, so the treatment becomes all the more difficult.

Because the symptoms of this disease are very general, it is suggested that you ask your veterinarian to conduct yearly tests for your pet.

This would help in detecting any issue in the very beginning, which makes it possible to treat it successfully.

Rotten skin

Octopuses shed the skin around the arms frequently. This will cause small flakes or pieces to float in the water. If these pieces are not removed, it can lead to rotten skin. The skin of the Octopus can also get infected by the bacteria on these skin pieces.

Octopuses tend to suffer from the issue of dry skin many a times. Dry skin is categorised by flaky skin. Some people mistake it for an infestation of algae.

If you attempt to look through the glass of the aquarium, you may see dry and loose flakes of skin. This is the main test of dry skin. There are a few causes that can lead to rotten skin, such as improper diet and dry surroundings.

Treatment:

You can also use olive oil capsules or vitamin E oil. These oils are easily available in all health stores. You can also put two to three drops in his food or water tank.

Continuous use of good quality oil will show you excellent results in a few weeks. Pour two to three drops of the oil at least once a week in the water tank of the pet.

It is also highly advised that you buy a mist humidifier. This will keep the water warm and humidity up. When an Octopus experiences low humidity levels, he can easily get dry skin.

If the problem does not end after all these measures, it is advised to get a skin scrape done by the veterinarian. This will help you to determine if there is more to the problem than what you understand.

Bacterial or fungal infection

Your Octopus can also be infected by yeast, bacterial or fungal infections. This can be very lethal so proper care should be taken.

In case you find the yeast infection symptoms, you should make it a point to take your pet to the vet. He will perform a stain test and confirm the presence or absence of the disease.

Causes:

There are many causes of the infection. The various causes that could be behind this health condition in your pet animal are as follows:

-   One of the main causes of any infection in Octopuses is lack of a healthy diet.

-   If your animal is on oral antibiotics, then it will have some side effect on the body of the Octopus. This infection could be one of the side effects of the oral antibiotics.

-   Another common cause of this health condition in Octopuses is stress. When your pet animal is going through excessive stress, it will lead to this health condition.

-   If there is poor hygiene around the Octopus, it can also lead to this health condition of infection. You should try to maintain optimum hygiene levels at all times.

- If the Octopus is suffering from some other infection or health condition, this infection could be a side effect of the health condition.

Symptoms:

There are certain symptoms that will help you to diagnose whether your Octopus has a yeast infection or not. In case you find the yeast infection symptoms, you should make it a point to take your pet to the vet. He will perform a gram stain test and confirm the presence or absence of the disease.

The following symptoms will help you to confirm whether your pet Octopus is suffering from this yeast infection:

- Do you smell something foul near your pet? If the answer is yes, then this could be the yeast infection.

- One of the early symptoms of this disease includes diarrhoea. If your pet is suffering from diarrhoea that you are not able to control, then your pet could be infected by this health condition.

- You should keep a check on the stools of the Octopus. The colour and texture of the stools will help you determine whether the Octopus has a bacterial infection or not.

- Does your Octopus suffer from frothy stools? Is the stool dark yellow or green in colour? If yes, then this could be a clear case of yeast infection, thrush.

- As the disease progresses, you will see more symptoms surface. The mouth of the Octopus can get very sore and dry.

- Another symptom that you will notice as the disease spreads is lesions. You should be on the lookout for this particular disease.

Treatment:

If your Octopus is suffering from thrush, you don't need to worry as it can be treated. It is advised to administer 0.1ml dose of antibiotic per one kilogram weight of the Octopus. Nilstat will effectively treat this yeast infection.

This is the dosage that is generally advised to treat most infections. You can even consult your veterinary before you give the dose to your pet.

When you are providing the treatment, there are certain precautions you need to take.

- After administering medicine, the pet might suffer from diarrhoea for a few days. This state can typically last for 2-3 days. Make sure that you take care of the pet's diet during this time because that will help him to revive from diarrhoea.

- The best way to administer medicine to the Octopus is to give each dose in between his feeds. This is the best way to help him fight against the diarrhoea.

- Another point that needs to be remembered is that you should never give the dose of medicine with the food that you serve the Octopus. There are many people who dissolve the dose in the water itself. This is not the right way because this will kill all the nutrition. The Octopus's health will only be harmed if you do something like this.

7. Senescence

It should be noted that an Octopus has no fat reserve. The Octopus can convert muscle to energy. During senescence body weight drops to almost half.

When you spot any of the given symptoms in your pet, you should know that something is not right. You will have to take a closer look at the pet and examine. This examination will help you to understand if there is something wrong with your pet.

While you are examining your pet, you should also understand that your pet could be scared. It is important that you make the pet feel comfortable. This will help you conduct the examination properly and without any problems.

You should make sure that you conduct the examination in a closed area, a place where the animal feels safe and protected. You should try to examine him indoors.

Do not let the place be crowded when the examination is being conducted. Make sure that all the other pets and your family members are outside and not in the same place where the examination is being conducted.

The noise level around you should be as low as possible. The noise will stress the pet and will irritate him, so make sure there is no noise around. Conduct the examination in a quiet place.

Be as gentle and kind as possible. This will help your pet to relax and feel less stressed. You should in no way add to the stress and pain of the pet.

If the animal will see you being fidgety, it will only add to his stress. You should be as calm and as confident as possible. Your confidence will give him some hope and relief.

You should check his entire body. Remember to check on both sides of the body. Start the examination at one particular point and then move ahead from that point. The examination should be definite and guided and not random.

Look at how your pet responds to the body examination being done. If you feel that the animal is not taking it too well, you should stop the examination. You should look for any stress signs that he displays. You should not ignore them; otherwise the animal can go into deep shock.

After administering medicine, the pet might suffer from diarrhoea for a few days. This state can typically last for 2-3 days. Make sure that you take care of the pet's diet during this time because that will help him to revive from diarrhoea.

The best way to administer medicine to the Octopus is to give each dose in between his feeds. This is the best way to help him fight against the diarrhoea.

Another point that needs to be remembered is that you should never give the dose of medicine with the food that you serve the Octopus. There are many people who dissolve the dose in the water itself. This is not the right way because this will kill all the nutrition. The Octopus's health will only be harmed if you do something like this.

8. Euthanasia

If you are still not aware of the procedure of euthanasia, then it is important that you understand the reasons that go behind euthanizing an Octopus, or any other animal for that matter. It is important that you understand that no one conducts this procedure for fun.

Euthanasia can put most people to a moral dilemma. There is always this question whether this is right or not. It is always advised that you should talk to doctors and other pet parents before you can take a decision of your own.

Chapter 8: Euthanasia of my pet Octopus

You might have to take the decision to euthanize your pet Octopus. It is important to understand that younger and smaller Octopuses can be easily euthanized with the help of ethanol. You might have to carry out a more elaborate procedure for older and bigger Octopuses.

Euthanasia has always been a subject of debate. Aquarists and doctors all over the world are always debating whether euthanasia is morally right or not. This decision lies with you. But, you should understand that sometimes there is no better way to relieve your pet.

Animal issues are no longer socially invisible. During the past half-century, efforts to ensure the respectful and humane treatment of animals have garnered global attention. Concern for the welfare of animals is reflected in the growth of animal welfare science and ethics.

The proliferation of interest in animal use and care at the national and international levels is also apparent in recent protections accorded to animals in new and amended laws and regulations, institutional and corporate policies, and purchasing and trade agreements.

The former is evident in the emergence of academic programs, scientific journals and funding streams committed either partially or exclusively to the study of how animals are impacted by various environments and human interventions.

Attention has also been focused on conservation and the impact of human interventions on terrestrial and aquatic wildlife and the environment. Within these contexts, stakeholders look to veterinarians to provide leadership on how to care well for animals, including how to relieve unnecessary pain and suffering.

Changing societal attitudes toward animal care and use have inspired scrutiny of some traditional and contemporary practices applied in the management of animals used for agriculture, research and teaching, companionship, and recreation or entertainment and of animals encountered in the wild.

The Guidelines set criteria for euthanasia, specify appropriate euthanasia methods and agents and are intended to assist veterinarians in their exercise of professional judgment. It is important to understand that euthanasia does not just involve death of the animal.

Euthanasia techniques essentially involve everything around it. It should take care of the pet before it is euthanized. It needs to take care of other details except just the death of the ailing pet animal.

Apart from delineating appropriate methods and agents, these guidelines also recognize the importance of considering and applying appropriate pre-euthanasia such as sedation and animal handling practices, as well as attention to disposal of animals' remains.

Motivational-effective neural networks also provide strong inputs to the limbic system, hypothalamus and autonomic nervous system for reflex activation of the pulmonary, cardiovascular and pituitary-adrenal systems.

Although the perception of pain requires a conscious experience, defining consciousness and therefore the ability to perceive pain, across many species is quite difficult.

Previously it was thought that fin fish, amphibians, reptiles, and invertebrates lacked the anatomic structures necessary to perceive pain as we understand it in birds and mammals.

For example, the invertebrate taxa include animals with no nervous system and nervous systems with no ganglion or minimal ganglion.

However, there are also invertebrate taxa with well-developed brains and complex behaviours that include the ability to analyse and respond to complex environmental cues such as Octopus, cuttlefish, spiders, honeybees, butterflies and ants.

1. Reasons to euthanize your Octopus

If you are still not aware of the procedure of euthanasia, then it is important that you understand the reasons that go behind euthanizing an Octopus, or any other animal for that matter. It is important that you understand that no one conducts this procedure for fun.

Euthanasia can put most people to moral dilemma. There is always this question whether this is right or not. It is always advised that you should talk to doctors and other pet parents before you can take a decision of your own.

Sometimes, there is no option left with the aquarists or the vet except to euthanize the Octopus. The following reasons some of the major reasons that go behind euthanizing an Octopus:

- **Health issues**: Bad health is generally one of the main reasons to conduct the procedure. Even if the pet is young, but very ill, the vet might euthanize him if there is no hope for his survival. In many such cases, the only way to relieve the Octopus or any other animal is to conduct the procedure of euthanasia on him.

- **Old age**: Old age is also a very common reason to euthanize an animal. Once the Octopus is old and incapable, it can get very difficult for him. If the vet feels that the pet's condition is only deteriorating, he might take the decision to conduct the procedure.

- **Lethargy**: Lethargy due to illness or age is a reason to euthanize. If the animal has become so lethargic that he can't go through most of his routine things, it can be very difficult for both the animal and the pet owner. In many such cases, the only way to relieve the Octopus or any other animal is to conduct the procedure of euthanasia on him.

2. Mechanisms of Euthanasia

It is important to understand euthanasia properly so that you don't have any doubts about the mechanism. Many a times, confusion of certain techniques leads to many misconceptions. You should try to save yourself from such misconceptions.

Debates that revolve around euthanasia also discuss whether the mechanisms involved in euthanasia are correct or not. Such debates have been going on for too long. Aquarists have different views.

It is advised that you learn about the various techniques and mechanisms involved. This knowledge will allow you to have a deeper understanding about this topic. You can understand what your Octopus will go through if you go opt for this technique.

When you are looking at ways to euthanize your old Octopus, you will definitely be hounded by the questions as to what are the various mechanisms of euthanasia. This section will help you understand these mechanisms.

Euthanizing agents cause death by three basic mechanisms:

- direct reduction or depression of the brain's neurons which are extremely critical for various life functions

- hypoxia

- The physical act of disruption of the entire brain activity.

The main aim of euthanasia is to reduce eliminate pain, distress and anxiety before the loss of consciousness.

As loss of consciousness resulting from these mechanisms can occur at different rates, the suitability of a particular agent or method will depend on whether an animal experiences distress prior to loss of consciousness.

It should be noted that unconsciousness is defined as loss of individual awareness. It occurs when the brain's ability to integrate information is blocked or disrupted. This should be the basic guideline for the veterinarian attempting euthanasia on your Octopus.

If you are looking at the most ideal situation where your pet experiences minimum distress then euthanasia methods should result in rapid loss of consciousness, followed by cardiac or respiratory arrest and the subsequent loss of brain function.

It should be noted here that loss of consciousness should precede loss of muscle movement.

Agents and methods that prevent movement through muscle paralysis but that do not block or disrupt the cerebral cortex or equivalent structures such as succinylcholine, nicotine, strychnine, curare, magnesium and potassium are not acceptable as sole agents for euthanasia.

If you are wondering as to why they are not allowed as sole agents then you should know that they can result in distress and conscious perception of pain prior to death.

On the other hand, magnesium salts are acceptable as the sole agent for euthanasia in many invertebrates due to the absence of evidence for cerebral activity in some members of these taxa.

Depending on the speed of onset of the particular agent or method used, release of inhibition of motor activity may be observed accompanied by vocalization and muscle contraction similar to that seen in the initial stages of anaesthesia.

Although distressing to observers, these responses does not appear to be purposeful.

Once ataxia and loss of righting reflex occurs, subsequent observed motor activity, such as convulsions, vocalization, and reflex struggling, can be attributed to the second stage of anaesthesia, which by definition lasts from the loss of consciousness to the onset of a regular breathing pattern.

Hypoxia is commonly achieved by exposing animals to high concentrations of gases that displace oxygen, such as carbon dioxide, nitrogen, or argon, or by exposure to carbon monoxide (CO) to block uptake of oxygen by red blood cells.

Exsanguination, an adjunctive method, is another method of inducing hypoxia and can be a way to ensure death in an already unconscious or moribund animal. It is important to note the reactions of the animal to the agent that is being introduced to him.

There are many euthanasia methods. A study on various animals has shown that some animals show a change in the motor activity after the agent is introduced. They might also show convulsions. This is generally followed by loss of consciousness, which is mainly due to hypoxia.

This is reflex activity and is not consciously perceived by the animal. In addition, methods based on hypoxia will not be appropriate for species that are tolerant of prolonged periods of hypoxemia.

When you are planning for your Octopus, it should be that you educate yourself well. It is known that animals presumably experience less fear and anxiety with methods that require little preparatory handling.

In contrast, administration of a local anaesthetic into the epidural space suppresses both spinally mediated nociceptive reflexes and ascending nociceptive pathways.

Noxious stimuli are not perceived as pain in conscious humans or nonhuman animals because activity in the ascending pathways, and thus access to the higher cortical centres, is suppressed or blocked.

It is incorrect to substitute the term pain for receptors, stimuli, pathways, or reflexes because the term implies higher sensory processing associated with conscious perception.

Consequently, the choice of a euthanasia agent or method is less critical if it is to be used on an animal that is anesthetized or unconscious, provided that the animal does not regain consciousness prior to death.

Physical methods must be executed properly. This is to ensure a quick and humane death because failure to do so can cause substantial suffering. In summary, the cerebral cortex or equivalent structure and subcortical structures must be functional for pain to be perceived.

We need to emphasize on knowledge and education. It is important that each person that plans to keep a cephalopod understand its life cycle.

It is important to understand the various reasons to conduct euthanasia. This information will go a long way in helping people keep Octopuses in the best possible way.

Conclusion

Thank you again for purchasing this book!

I hope this book was able to help you in understanding the various ways to domesticate and care for an Octopus.

A pet is like a family member. It is more than important that you take care of all the responsibilities for the animal. It is important to have a thorough understanding about the animal. Spend some time to get to know everything about the Octopus. This will help you know your pet better. The more you know about your pet, the better bond you will form with him. Whenever you bring a pet home, you have to make sure that you are all ready for the responsibilities ahead.

If you wish to raise an Octopus as a pet, there are many things that you need to keep in mind. It can be very daunting for a new owner. Because of the lack of information, you will find yourself getting confused as to what should be done and what should be avoided. You might be confused and scared. But, there is no need to feel so confused. After you learn about the Octopuses, you will know how adorable they are. You should equip yourself with the right knowledge.

An Octopus is an adorable pet that will keep you busy and entertained by all its unique antics. It is said that each animal is different from the other. Each one will have some traits that are unique to him. It is important to understand the traits that differentiate the Octopus from other aquarium animals. You also have to be sure that you can provide for the animal. So, it is important to be acquainted with the dos and don'ts of keeping the Octopus.

It is important that you understand the basic behaviour of the animal. This will help you to understand what lies ahead of you. If you understand how the animal should be cared for, you will make it work for yourself. You should aim at learning about the animal and then doing the right thing for him. This will help you to form a relationship with him.

If you are still contemplating whether you want to domesticate the Octopus or not, then it becomes all the more important for you to understand everything regarding the pet very well. You can only make a wise decision when you are acquainted will all these and more. When you are planning to domesticate an Octopus as a pet, you should lay special emphasis on learning about its behaviour, habitat requirements, diet requirements and common health issues.

When you decide to domesticate an animal, it is important that you understand the animal and its species well. It is important to learn the basic nature and mannerisms of the animal. This book will help you to equip yourself with this knowledge. You will be able to appreciate the Octopuses for what they are. You will also know what to expect from the animal. This will help you to decide whether the Octopus is the right choice for you or not. If you already have the pet, then this book will help you to strengthen your bond with your pet.

The ways and strategies discussed in the book are meant to help you get acquainted with everything that you need to know about Octopuses. You will be able to understand the unique antics of the animal. This will help you to decide whether the Octopus is suitable to be your pet. The book teaches you simple ways that will help you to understand your pet. This will allow you take care of your pet in a better way. You should be able to appreciate your pet and also care for the animal with the help of the techniques discussed in this book.

Thank you and good luck!

References

Note: at the time of printing, all the websites below were working. As the internet changes rapidly, some sites might no longer be live when you read this book. That is, of course, out of our control.

https://www.tonmo.com

https://www.pets4homes.co.uk

http://www.tfhmagazine.com

https://www.mnn.com

http://www.advancedaquarist.com

http://www.nationalgeographic.com

www.ehow.co.uk

http://animals.mom.me

https://en.wikipedia.org

https://www.lovethatpet.com

https://www.thespruce.com

https://www.bluecross.org.uk

https://pethelpful.com

http://www.seniorlink.co.nz

http://www.drsfostersmith.com

www.bbc.co.uk

https://www.cuteness.com

http://www.aquarium-pond-answers.com

http://jacksonville.com

http://www.arkive.org

http://www.vetstreet.com

https://www.hillsborovet.com

www.training.ntwc.org

www.wildlifehealth.org

http://animaldiversity.org

https://www.yourpetspace.info

http://healthypets.mercola.com

https://www.finecomb.com

https://a-z-animals.com

https://www.theguardian.com

http://www.businessinsider.com

https://www.saltwaterfish.com

http://runescape.wikia.com

https://www.wired.com

http://www.kijiji.ca

https://blogs.scientificamerican.com

http://www.huffingtonpost.ca

https://www.gumtree.com

http://www.marshallpet.com

https://www.petplace.com

https://yourfishstore.com

59969526R00061

Made in the USA
Columbia, SC
10 June 2019